Amazon FBA:

A Step-by-Step Business guide for beginners to have the right mastery. Learn the retail sail, have successful and know everything about online arbitrage.

Table of Contents

Introduction

What is FBA?

FBA, or Fulfillment by Amazon, is an easy way to get your products delivered to your customers. You just have to send the products you list on the website to an Amazon warehouse, and they take it from there. Amazon gives your products more visibility, and it's an easy way to earn more. You don't have to deal with the trouble of packaging and shipping, and you get Amazon's name backing your product.

Amazon has various fulfillment centers set up at many places in the country, and all you have to do is send your inventory to these centers. You have to pay for the storage and handling of products. Whenever you receive an order, Amazon will take care of the packaging and shipping for you. When it's delivered to the customer, you'll get a notification from Amazon. Even most of the customer service is handled by Amazon if an issue arises. This helps you take your business to higher levels without putting in too much effort.

Advantages of Amazon FBA

Amazon's large customer base provides an outstanding marketplace for people who want to effortlessly market products or services online to a large group of people. The majority of Amazon customers prefer to purchase products that can be shipped to them via FBA. Amazon, in fact, claims that most customers buy items from a third-party vendor only if the product or service they are providing is Amazon trusted, meaning Fulfilled by Amazon. FBA allows you to target two specific groups of people who might otherwise dismiss your listings due to shipping costs.

Great Customer Service

One of the greatest things that Amazon is known for is their customer support. Whether or not they get back to their customers quickly about an issue with a product or they promise quick delivery regardless of what day of the week, Amazon always lets their customers know that they are the priority in their line of work. They want your customers to feel that way too when they purchase something while on the Amazon website.

Customers Eligible for Super Saver Shipping

All online buyers who buy products worth at least $25 are eligible for free Super Saver Shipping. These are shoppers who will typically not pay extra for shipping even if a non-FBA seller offers a product at a lower price. However, such customers don't mind spending an extra dollar or two in order to earn Super Shipping Service.

Customers who Subscribe to Prime Membership

Prime Membership guarantees free two-day delivery on all products shipped directly from Amazon's warehouse. By paying the annual Prime membership fee, these customers are making a direct investment in FBA. As a result, they receive their items sooner than if they had purchased them from a potentially lower-priced third-party vendor. All Prime members are awarded free shipping service for one year until they renew their membership.

Your Job as a Seller will be Simpler and Effortless

FBA makes the process of selling items easy. Simply gather your merchandise, enter the details of your items online and email the details to the fulfillment center. Amazon will then help you find buyers, list your items on a dashboard, safely store your items in its warehouses and ship the products to your customers. Furthermore, Amazon will handle customer service. While Amazon is taking care of all the marketing/shipping details, you can then focus your time on your business strategy.

Generate HUGE Profits

In today's highly competitive market, it's not easy to attract business. With millions of people trying to sell their products online and offline, you need to have an edge in the market. Amazon FBA offers you that edge, providing a platform that gives shoppers concrete incentives for choosing FBA items over non-FBA ones. These shoppers have the potential to become loyal customers who don't mind paying a little extra in order to quickly receive quality products or quality services.

Less Competition in a Highly Competitive Marketplace

When you're trying to set a price for your product on Amazon, you don't have to compete with other non-FBA players selling similar items. Your customers will be aware of the quality of service you are offering through Amazon FBA. Price your merchandise fairly and you'll stay competitive—without compromising the profit margins.

Less Overhead Costs

Compare the difference in costs when it comes to shipping your products directly to customers versus using FBA. Do the analysis and you'll discover that shipping your items directly to shoppers requires more packaging material than is required when you use FBA. This may seem like a small expense, but ship enough merchandise and such an expense (or saving) adds up fast.

You Become More Visible in the Marketplace

When a shopper searches the site for a product, the website brings up search results in ascending order of price, with the least expensive at the top of the list. Amazon.com shows its customers the total price, including base price and cost of shipping. Since FBA provides free shipping, the base price that is listed will not factor in shipping costs. Therefore, your items will always appear higher in the search results, improving the visibility of your listed items.

Seamless Customer Experience for Your Clients

Unless you have a dedicated customer service staff, you can't attend to your customers' needs 24/7, much as you might want to. Customer service is another one of the extremely important business details that requires an extensive investment of time. Amazon FBA can provide that 24-hour service, giving you peace of mind as you attend to other important aspects of your business.

Continue Doing Business Even When Not Physically Present

Perhaps you've encountered a situation where you had to temporarily close your Amazon shop and/or had to deactivate product listings because you could not be immediately available to pack and ship your merchandise. You want customers to get their purchases immediately, and any kind of delay is unacceptable. FBA gives you peace of mind. As you take care of other important matters, rest assured that your packages will be sold and shipped in a timely fashion.

Growth Prospects

When it comes to e-retailing, Amazon is the industry leader. Amazon's business is snowballing and will continue to do so. If you are looking for maximum exposure and action, then Amazon is a good choice for you.

Disadvantages of Amazon FBA

Although Amazon FBA is an amazing platform with plenty of wonderful features, there are definitely things to consider as far as disadvantages go. Amazon FBA can have drawbacks that make the platform somewhat challenging to navigate, or that perhaps make it take longer for newcomers to learn how to use the platform efficiently. Recognizing these disadvantages in advance can help you determine if you are willing to deal with these disadvantages. It can also help you prepare and plan for them so that they do not pose a significant risk for you in the future by making you an informed business owner.

Difficult to Track Inventory

First things first, it can be somewhat difficult to track and manage inventory with Amazon FBA if you are not aware of how to use the system. Although Amazon does their best to keep everything updated and organized through their own tracking system, if you are not creating your own tracking system, it can be a hassle to know what needs to be ordered and when.

The best way to navigate this disadvantage is to set up a system for you to manage and monitor your products on a consistent basis. This way, when your products are in need of being ordered again, you know what needs to be ordered, when, and how many. Remember, at the end of the day, Amazon's systems are for Amazon. They use their tracking and inventory management systems as a tool to help their fulfillment employees find the products that they need to fulfill orders. You are going to need to come up with your own way of tracking and managing inventory so that you can fulfill your own needs, such as keeping popular items in stock and ordering new products.

Potential Increase in Returns

Amazon FBA offers an easy returns policy so that if your client does not like what they have ordered, they can easily return it for a refund. When you run your own Amazon shop, you are able to choose your return policies and, generally, it is more challenging to facilitate returns anyway because you are using smaller, private shipping companies. This means that returns are generally not facilitated because people are not interested in dealing with the more complex return policy that smaller merchants offer. With Amazon FBA, however, the easy return is a part of their Amazon Prime feature, and more people tend to use it due to how easy it is.

This increase in ease could mean an increase in product returns, particularly if you are selling products that are low in quality or that are inaccurately described on your platform. This means that you could have a harder time selling out of products and maintaining your sales if you are not careful. The best way to mitigate this risk is to ensure that you are always checking for quality and selling high-quality products to your customers and that the descriptions are accurate. This way, you are less likely to get returns.

Additional Expenses and Fees

All of the added benefits of Amazon FBA certainly do come with increased fees and expenses. As we discussed previously, there are certain fee structures and schedules that you are going to have to work with in order to use this platform to run your business. Of course, for many people, all of the added convenience is well worth the investment, especially since you are likely still going to come out profitable in the end anyway. Although it may cut into your profits somewhat, it may turn out to be cheaper in the long run due to you not having to spend so much on your own inventory storage and shipping fees.

Difficult Shipping Prep

Until you learn how, navigating the shipping process of getting your products from your supplier to the Amazon FBA warehouse facilities can be fairly challenging. First, you need to discover which facility you are to ship your products so that you can get your products there in the first place. This way, you can give your supplier the right information to get your products to the Amazon FBA facilities. Then, you also have to make sure that your products are compliant and that they are registered with Amazon to be received. If your products are not compliant and if they have the wrong identification codes on them, Amazon will deny the shipment and send it back to your supplier. This can lead to a costly and lengthy process of getting your products sent back to Amazon again with the proper product codes registered this time.

The first few times you go through the process can be challenging which can make this probably one of the more difficult learning curves of having an Amazon FBA store to begin with. Once you navigate this process a few times, however, you will find that it becomes easier. All you have to be extra cautious about is product codes to avoid having shipments denied by Amazon when they reach the facility.

Greater Competition

Amazon does do a great deal of work to drive customers to their website, but it doesn't mean that they are driving their customers to your shop. Unless, of course, your shop is relevant and has a high positive rating with your clients, in which case Amazon will rank you higher in their algorithm. At the end of the day, Amazon wants to get their customers into the best merchants' shops so that they can purchase great products and have a positive experience. This is what will provide Amazon with return customers which in turn provides their merchants like you with return customers. Naturally, you are going to be driving customers to your shop too through your own efforts, but this is generally how it works on Amazon.

Possible Reduced Perceived Value

This lower perceived value that tends to come along with Amazon's reputation often comes from the fact that there are many merchants selling counterfeit products or knock-offs, as well as many who source low-quality products from cheap overseas suppliers.

Although you can certainly source from cheaper overseas suppliers, it is up to you as the merchant to make sure that the products you are getting are still valuable enough to be purchased and kept by your audience. If you are not being cautious about this, you might find yourself having a lot of returns and losing your own reputation right from the beginning by being a low quality, careless merchant on Amazon.

The best way to offset this disadvantage is to build a brand for yourself and set yourself apart from day one. Make sure that you put effort into having quality products, and make sure that your customers see this effort being made so that they know that you are taking pride in your store. This way, they are going to see that you have a high-quality store and, because of that, they will trust in your store and likely choose your products over anyone else's.

Chapter 1: How FBA Functions

Understanding FBA and its functioning is really easy. All you have to do is send your inventory to an Amazon Fulfillment Center, and from there on the Amazon people take care of it. They'll handle all the back-end operations. They do everything from storing inventory to fulfilling orders to handling customer support and order returns. They're very consistent about it, which improves your reliability as a seller. It's totally up to you how much you want to store, according to your finances.

Here's how you register for FBA:

1)   Open the following URL on your web browser: www.amazon.com/fba.

2)   Click on "Get Started."

3)   You don't have to register for a Seller Central account since you already have one. You just have to select "Add FBA to your account".

4)   Then log into your Seller Central account and check the Inventory tab.

5) Click on the "Manage Inventory" option and choose which products you would like to list for FBA. There's a checkbox next to each product and you can mark it to list it for FBA.

6) Once you've selected all the products you want to list, click on the Actions drop-down menu, and select "Change to Fulfilled by Amazon."

7) On the next page, click on "Convert."

After this, you have to ready your stock and send it to an Amazon Fulfillment Center. Here are the instructions for doing that:

1) Go to your account's Inventory tab.

2) Click on "Manage Inventory" and once again, mark the checkboxes against the items you want to go for FBA.

3) Then click on the Actions drop-down menu, and select "Send/Replenish Inventory."

4) Then you'll be asked to give a ship address. Provide the necessary details.

5) You will be asked how you're going to ship the products: case-packed or individual items.

Note: Before you do this, make sure to take a look at the Dangerous Units, Hazardous Materials, and EBA Prohibited Products page, to be sure everything is legal.

The next step is to review the labeling requirements. Amazon's receiving systems are dependent on barcodes; so all units you send to them must be tagged with a barcode that is able to be scanned. There are three ways to do this:

1)   Manually print and apply labels to each unit.

2)   Use the Label Service from FBA itself. Everything will be handled by Amazon.

3)   If your products are eligible, sign up for the Stickerless Commingled Inventory.

Here are Amazon's recommendations for when you are preparing to print labels for your products:

• Use a laser or a thermal printer and avoid inkjet printers. This will decrease chances of fading and smearing.

• Your printer should be able to handle resolutions above 300DPI.

• Make sure you're using the right print media.

- Regularly clean and replace your printer heads.

- Test your labels periodically by scanning them yourself. See if they're legible.

You will receive a PDF file once you have entered the number of units you'll be shipping for each product. You can print these labels later. Again, there are some guidelines:

- Use white label stock with removable adhesive to print the labels. This makes them easily scannable and removable.

- Make sure only product label that Amazon provided is visible. If there are other barcodes on your product/package, hide them all properly.

- Some products require prepping before they are shipped, which can slow down the shipping process. To avoid this, you can use FBA Prep Services. You can also send them fully prepped to the fulfillment centers.

- Each box sent to Amazon should have a unique shipping label. It's the only way to identify it at the fulfillment center.

Here are your guidelines for attaching the labels:

• Don't place the labels on a place where they'll be cut. Try to place them in the middle of the box if possible. Never place them on the seams or corners.

• There must be a unique shipping label on each box.

• If there are pallets, each one has to have five labels. One goes on the top and the others go on each side.

When all of this is done, schedule a time for the pickup of your inventory. Mark all the items you are shipping as "Shipped" in the Shipment Summary. From there on, you can track the status of your shipment in the Shipping Queue. Allow a period of at least 24 hours before checking whether the status is updated to "Delivered." After that, you can contact your carrier to confirm delivery.

"Checked-In" means that some part of your shipment has reached, and they're waiting for the rest. Once the barcode scanning starts; the status again changes to "Receiving." The whole process usually takes about six days, so be patient. After this, the dimensions of all your products are recorded. Once they're stored, they can be shipped anytime.

Amazon's web-to-warehouse picking system is very advanced. It can sort through inventories in the warehouse really fast and when a customer purchases something, it will pick the right method of shipping them the product according to their preference. The order can be accurately tracked by the customer throughout the shipping process. This makes for a very pleasant experience for the customer.

Chapter 2: Mindset for success

How to Have the Right Mindset

We will talk about what you should be doing to make sure that you are not failing in your endeavors to start this Amazon FBA to live a healthier life overall. This chapter will show you what you could be doing to make this Amazon FBA your lifestyle and to not only help you to start the Amazon FBA and stay on track, but also to live with this plan for the rest of your life. These daily patterns will help you to not fail with your Amazon FBA. We understand that you may fail a couple of times in any Amazon FBA, and it is understandable to do so. Nonetheless, this chapter will show you how to make sure you are consistent and not failing. These habits have been followed by many successful people to get optimal results in all of their aspects of life, whether it is fitness related or anything else. Make sure you start implementing all these habits after you are done reading this book as it will help you to make this Amazon FBA your lifestyle. The reason why this chapter might sound philosophical is that the only way you will see success with this Amazon FBA is if you do it consistently. For you to do that, you need to change your current lifestyle by being more productive and disciplined. You have to remember that healthy eating is for more than just an Amazon FBA; it's a lifestyle.

Plan your day ahead

Planning your day ahead of time is crucial, Not only does planning out your day help you be more prepared for your day moving forward, but it will also help you to become more aware of the things you shouldn't be doing, hence That are wasting your time.

Moreover, planning your day will truly help you with making the most out of your time. That being said, we will talk about two things:

- Benefits of planning out your day

- How to go about planning out your day

So, without further ado, let us dive into the benefits of planning out your day.

It will help you prioritize

Yes, planning out your day will help you prioritize a lot of things in your day-to-day life. You can allocate time limits to the things you want to work on the most to least, for example, if you're going to write your book and you are super serious about it. Then you need a specific time limit every day in which you work on a task wholeheartedly without any worries of other things until the time is up. Then you move on to the next job in line, so when you schedule out your whole day and you give yourself time limits, then you can prioritize your entire day. The same thing goes for your Amazon FBA, make sure you allocate time for prepping your plans for the next day, which will allow you to have goals ready for you when you need it, hence making it easy for you to continue on with your Amazon FBA.

More focus on the task on hand

This point is quite similar to the previous point, as once you have started to plan out your day you have become more aware of the things that you are about to do. With the time limit on all tasks that you do daily, it will create an urgency to get as much of the job done as you can before time is up and you are moving on to your next appointment. Which will help you be more focused on the task at hand and get more things done. Many people consider planning your day out to be time-consuming, which it isn't if you prioritize your time the right way. If you plan your goals the day before, then it should not be a problem.

Work-Life Balance

You see, once you start planning out your whole day, you become more aware of your time and how to balance it out. Once you begin to write out your entire day ahead of you, you will know precisely what you are doing that day so you don't have to do anything sporadically throughout the day. Always plan some time for yourself every day where you can wind down, read a good book, meditate, or maybe hang out with your friends. You will feel refreshed the next day. Having to wind down and "chill out" will only make you a more productive person.

Planning out your whole day ahead will not only help you prioritize better. It will also help you be more focused on your task on hand and will help you have a better work-life balance. This will help you to stay motivated with the Amazon FBA that you are following. So now that we have discovered the benefits of planning out your day, let's dive into the how-to's when it comes to planning out your day.

Summarize your Normal Day

Now, before we start getting into planning out your whole day, you need to realize that to plan your entire day, you need to know precisely what you are doing that day. Which means you need to write down every single thing you do on a typical day and write down the time you start and end. It needs to be detailed in terms of how long it takes for your transportation to get to work, etc.

Now after you have figured out your whole day, you can decide how to prioritize your day. It could be cutting out a task that you don't require or shortening your time for a job that doesn't need that much time. After you have your priorities for the day, you can add pleasurable tasks into your day like hanging out with your friends, etc.

Chapter 3: Find the right product to sell

This is without a doubt the most important step in starting a business on the Amazon FBA program. Everything will be dependent on how well you perform in this step. As you should know, Amazon is the biggest marketplace online. Almost anything that you can think of is being sold on the site. Let's perform a quick exercise. Off the top of your head, think of a really absurd product. Then do a quick search for it on the Amazon website. I bet your search will generate dozens if not hundreds of product listings. My point here is that literally everything under the sun is being sold on Amazon.

This brings me to my next point which is "competition". Because of the immense number of goods being offered for sale on Amazon, the competition among sellers is just as immense. You may have a good product in your hands but if you are up against cutthroat competition, then you have very little chance in moving forward. This is why it's important that you do your research first before you start selling on Amazon. You need to look for products that have a market but aren't too competitive. To simplify things, your product should meet two factors:

1. There's a demand for it.

2. Only a few people are selling it on Amazon.

You have to keep in mind that not all products can be sold via the Amazon FBA program. There are goods that are simply too cumbersome to sell on the platform. There are certain attributes that you should look for in a product that makes it a viable Amazon FBA item. The most important of such attributes are as follows.

a. It has to be lightweight and small. Remember that you will be shipping the items to one of Amazon's fulfillment centers. The bigger and heavier the items are, the more expenses you will spend on shipping and storage. The general rule is that your product should be able to fit snugly into a flat-rate box. It should not weigh more than one or two pounds.

b. It should be unregulated. Or it could be regulated but the rules are not that stringent. The problem in selling regulated products like batteries, toys, and food is that they come with red tape which makes them hard to sell because you need to go through a lot of paperwork and certifications. For example, if you are going to sell toys for children, you have to acquire several approvals and certifications to prove that your toys do not pose health hazards to kids.

c. The products should be non-seasonal. This basically means that you can sell the products in any season. It doesn't matter if it's January or July or December. Demand for the product should be all year round. Examples of seasonal products are Christmas lights, Valentine's Day cards, Halloween costumes. These are products that you should avoid because demand for them are very seasonal.

d. The products should be uncomplicated. You can just ship them to the fulfillment centers with little worries. A mouse pad is a good example of an uncomplicated product. Electronic gadgets are examples of complicated products. Electronics may be fun to sell but they come with a ton of headaches and customer service issues. They have so many moving parts. What if a customer wants to replace a part? What if the customer can't find the appropriate batteries for it? Keep in mind that you are selling dozens if not hundreds of these products. Imagine if a good number of your customers find issues with the products. You will be inundated with dozens of emails and inquiries.

To help you with your research, here are some very practical tips on how to look for good products to sell through the Amazon FBA program:

1. Dig through the departments and sub-categories within Amazon to look for new products and new releases. Your first step in your product research should be within the Amazon website itself. Browse through the site's various departments, categories, and sub-categories. You can get dozens of product ideas by

scrolling through the listings. Keep notes on the products that catch your attention. Jot them down on a pad paper so that you can get back on them later on for more in-depth research. The great thing about product listings within Amazon's departments and categories is that you can sort the products using various criteria like popularity, price range, date of release, and average reviews. Looking into these information can help you decide if it's worth it to pursue a particular product or not.

2. Look into what other people are selling through the Amazon FBA program. This is very easy to do. It's the same as what we have discussed above in number one but you focus on products that are specifically being sold by entrepreneurs enrolled in the FBA program. You can determine which products are getting a lot of sales based on the number of reviews they get and how well they rank in the search results. Look at these products, look at the people selling them, and try to understand why they are very successful in the platform. Your main objective here is to identify the things that they are doing right and see if you can replicate them.

3. Take advantage of Jungle Scout. This is an extension for the Chrome browser which makes it very easy for you to perform product research on Amazon. All you have to do is do a query on Amazon for a particular product idea. When the search results finish loading, you simply click on the Jungle Scout button on the right side of your browser's address bar. The extension will provide you with valuable information about the product such as average reviews per product, average monthly sales, and price fluctuations. Of course, you can only use the Jungle Scout extension if you purchased and downloaded it. Yes, it comes with a price but it's completely worth it.

4. Get ideas from Google Trends. This is a free service by Google which shows you the topics and queries that are very popular among users of the search engine. The service shows you what topics are trending, what topics are increasing in popularity, what topics are losing steam. These are usually shown alongside simple graphs so that you can easily understand and sometimes predict the direction of a trend. These trends can help you brainstorm for product ideas. For example, if the topic healthy food is trending, this means you need to think about products that might

fulfill the needs of people who are searching for information about healthy food products.

5. Stay away from departments and categories on Amazon that are dominated by global brands. It's usually a waste of time trying to compete with the big brands. They have established themselves on Amazon and often times, you can't compete with them when it comes to price no matter how good your products are. So if you are doing product research on Amazon and you learn that big companies are already selling the products you have in mind, you should move on and look for other ideas.

6. Look for evergreen products. Evergreen is a term used to describe products that are in demand no matter the time of the year. It basically means that the product is not seasonal. People are buying it from January to December. Good examples of evergreen products are common household items, standard apparel like shirts and jeans, books, art supplies, etc. These are goods that are in demand throughout the year. If you want to run an Amazon FBA business that's profitable all year round, then you should only sell evergreen products.

7. Get product ideas using a keyword research tool. A keyword research tool is an online application that enables you to analyze sets and groups of keywords and keyword phrases. It's a powerful way to look for suggestions related to your product idea. For example, let's say that you plan on selling leather sandals on Amazon FBA. Using a keyword research tool, you can find many keywords that are relevant to the term "leather sandals". You might come across relevant keywords like "leather sandals for children", "leather hiking sandals", "leather house sandals", or "leather slippers". You may not eventually use these additional keywords but they can provide you with really good product ideas that you can pursue in your next project or next online campaign.

8. Find products that you can sell at higher margins. Selling a $2 toy at $5 is better than selling a $300 camera at $301. At first glance, it seems like selling a $300 camera is more lucrative and more profitable than selling a $2 toy. But if you look at the revenue per item, the toy earned $3 while the camera earned only $1. What I am trying to say here is that you should look for low-cost products that you can resell at high

margins. Don't make the mistake of assuming that higher-priced items will net you more profits.

9. Do product research in other online marketplaces like eBay or Clickbank. Or you can browse the websites of major retailers like Walmart and Target to see what types of products are selling like hotcakes in their platforms. You go through the sites the way you go through Amazon. Look at the popular products. Look at what the biggest sellers are doing. Find out which products are getting the most reviews. Crunch through the information and see if you can sell the same products on Amazon.

In using these strategies in product research, you should be able to come up with the right products for your FBA business. Take your time with your research. Don't rush because rushing is often the culprit behind ill-planned products. You don't have to use all of the research strategies I have discussed in this chapter. Just use the ones that work well for your business and niche.

Chapter 4: Find a Supplier to Source your Products

Now you have a product in mind that you can sell and it's time to obtain a supplier or manufacturing company that can source products at a wholesale price and brand them under your private label.

You can either source your items from another country or get them from manufacturers that operate domestically (based in the country where you operate). There are pros and cons.

The Pros of Outsourcing:

- Great item selection to choose from.

- Products can be made at very low prices.

- It is not difficult to identify a supplier who can manufacture the product you want to sell.

- Suppliers are ready to work for anyone who pays them.

The Cons of Outsourcing:

- Substantial shipping charges may be applicable.

- Customers may not understand the actual value of the product.

- Shipping increases wait time.

- There are more chances of things not going as planned, due to communication gaps.

When you evaluate both sides, you will see that sourcing products overseas seem to be a better way due to the quality of the product and the lower manufacturing costs. You can deal with the language barrier by choosing a country where people can understand your language. If you are able to find a supplier who is ready to make the product for you at competitive prices, by all means, go with that manufacturer.

Why Your Products Should Be Manufactured in China

Manufacturing your products in any other country can be really daunting due to culture and language barriers. But even then, the benefits of getting the products manufactured in China certainly overshadow these barriers. You can easily overcome the language barrier as most manufacturers (at least the famous ones, as they have to deal with English-speaking clients often) will have a representative who can speak and understand English.

Chinese manufacturing offers:

• Better service: This is particularly important for all beginners as initially, they will be looking at placing small orders and hence very few manufacturers will be interested in doing business with them. Chinese manufacturers, however, will.

• Better output: Believe it or not, there are hardly any manufacturers in China who cannot deliver what you are looking for—whether it is big or small. Also, when they commit to being ready with your order within a specific time frame, there are high chances that they will do so. In most of the cases, local manufacturers take you for granted and ask for more time.

• Ability to duplicate products: Chinese manufacturers are extremely good at creating something unique from an existing idea; they do not have to start from scratch. Suppose you are manufacturing yoga mats and you really like the texture and design of xyz yoga mats available in the market. You show the product to the manufacturer and ask them to give your product the same design and texture. Trust me, you won't be disappointed when you see the results.

Now, the next question is how to find suppliers. To keep things simple and straightforward, let's consider Alibaba, which specializes in global wholesale trading of products with most of its manufacturers based in China, India and across Southeast Asia.

Sourcing Your Products using Alibaba

Alibaba, an online marketplace founded in 1999 that connects suppliers and manufacturers around the globe, is where businesses go to inexpensively source their products in bulk so that they can private label them or resell them. Alibaba first originated in China. Though it has suppliers from other parts of the world too, it is essentially China's version of Amazon.

Sellers looking to sell their products on Amazon can find virtually anything on Alibaba including apparel, kitchenware, toys and footwear. One of the biggest advantages of using Alibaba is that both sellers and buyers can browse through their huge database of manufacturers, suppliers and products.

Alibaba makes it simple for you to find suppliers who are willing to work with you quickly and efficiently to create your product. The website also helps its users by offering certain measures to ensure that you work only with trusted partners, ensuring you are never scammed.

Look for Your Product

The first step in the process of finding a supplier who can source your product is to look for your product. This should bring you to a big list of suppliers who can possibly help you make your item. Filters such as Gold Supplier, Assessed Supplier, etc. help you find only legitimate suppliers. You also have an option to filter the results based on Location and Minimum Order.

Generally, it's advisable to use the Trade Assurance and Gold Supplier filters to find authentic suppliers. However, it's helpful to understand what each of these filters does so that you can use them effectively and efficiently.

Trade Assurance – This filter provides a free guarantee of an assessment of product quality prior to shipment as well as on-time shipment. Particularly when you have stringent deadlines, it's a useful filter, specifically designed to build trust between suppliers and buyers on Alibaba. You are covered if your products are not shipped on time or if the quality of your product does not meet the standards agreed to in the contract.

Gold Supplier – By selecting this filter, Alibaba shows only suppliers who are prequalified on the website, paying an annual fee to be tagged as Gold Suppliers. If you apply this filter while looking for suppliers, it should show you only the genuine ones, but there is a slight chance that some non-authentic suppliers could be mistagged. Therefore, it's preferable not rely on just this filter to eliminate poor suppliers—always use multiple filters along with your own knowledge.

On-site Check – This filter gives you a list of suppliers who have had their business' authenticity verified by Alibaba. If a supplier has an on-site check enabled, it means he/she is a genuine and trusted supplier.

Assessed Supplier – This filter offers the highest level of authentication that a supplier can ever attain on Alibaba. All those who have this tag have been verified by an inspection agency that has evaluated their operations in order to approve this label.

Location – This filter lets you source your product from a supplier who is located anywhere. So, you can filter out your results based on this filter. For example, some sellers on Amazon like to see if there are suppliers based in America to manufacture their product. If not, they can select another region.

Minimum Order – The Minimum Order filter lets you select the size of your minimum order. For instance, if you want the order to be less than 100, you can enter 100 in the Minimum Order box so that it lists suppliers that can give you a minimum order quantity of less than 100. This is particularly useful when you are looking only for suppliers who can give you the number of units you are looking to buy. Do not just go by the number they mention on their product page, as some of them do say they have x number as a Minimum Order Quantity, but even then they are okay to work with you based on your preferences.

Most people generally opt to use the Gold Supplier filter as it does a good job of filtering out spam. Some businesses also choose to use Trade Assurance as this is also a great filter to ensure you are dealing with only trusted suppliers. The best thing to do is to check all the filters while doing the product search for the first time. This way you are increasing the possibility of finding only legitimate supplies. Based on the type of item you have decided to sell, you might or might not find suppliers if you apply all the filters. If your product is popular among suppliers, you might see a couple of listings and you might not have too many options. If this is the case, start unchecking the filters you have applied, starting with the Assessed Supplier filter as this is the toughest one to find when it comes to suppliers.

Once you uncheck the Assessed Supplier filter, you should be able to see a good number of suppliers for your product. If you still do not see too many options, begin unchecking other filters until you find one, but try to keep the Gold Supplier filter on.

Different Sections of the Product Page

If you are using Alibaba for the first time, it's helpful to familiarize yourself with different sections on the product page.

Search Bar – This is the area where you can search for manufacturers or products you are interested in. Note: there is a drop-down box on the left side of the search bar, and here you can refine your search for Products, Quotes or Suppliers.

Sourcing Solutions – This drop-down menu offers many options to users so that they can easily refine their search. Suppliers can be efficiently searched for by submitting a buying request, region, type of stocks, global expos and so on.

Pictures – This is quite self-explanatory as it shows you images of the listed products. If there are good quality images of the product, you can see that the supplier cares enough to offer details to his customers.

Free On-Board Price – FOB, or Free on Board, gives you the cost range that is required to create one unit. Note: this price will be different from what you will be offered by the suppliers as this is just a rough estimate. After adding various components, the cost will increase.

Minimum Order Quantity (MOQ) – MOQ, or Minimum Order Quantity, gives the minimum number of units per order. For instance, with a specific brand of toy where the minimum order quantity is 1500 units, the supplier will take orders only when the minimum number is 1500. Note: although many suppliers mention a high MOQ for their orders, they may be open to lowering it if you make the request. Talk to them before making any decision.

Supply Ability – This gives you a rough estimate of how much the supplier can produce in a month. This is not that helpful as good suppliers should be able to supply as many products as you need.

Payment Options – Although there are several payment methods available, it is always good to weigh the pros and cons to understand which one works the best. Here are the most common payment methods along with information about the associated risk level for each:

• Bank Transfer: With bank transfers, the supplier receives the money upfront (even before production starts). This method is quite risky and is therefore not recommended for new sellers. Even if you are not new, a bank transfer is not a good option unless you know the supplier. Once the payment is made, and you are not happy with what has been delivered to you, there is little you can do about it. Risk level: High

• Letter of Credit: This is a fairly safe option and works out well for both the buyers and suppliers. However, this method involves some complex procedures and is recommended only for big orders. Risk level: Low

• PayPal: PayPal is a well-known payment method that is typically used by those who offer or receive services from individuals/companies overseas. PayPal is quite easy to use and presents a safe payment method for buyers as it has a good level of buyer protection. Although it is popular with buyers, it is not as popular among the suppliers due to high tax rates, difficulties with withdrawals and other chargebacks from dishonest buyers. Risk level: Fairly safe

• Western Union: Western Union is seen as a risky option for buyers and is not recommended when buyers' payments are not protected through escrow. Buyers can use this if they know the sellers well, but there is no rescue for them if things do not turn out to be the way they had assumed. Risk level: Very high

• Escrow: Escrow service is offered by several companies that are ready to hold the payment for the two parties. In this payment method, a buyer's money is held by a third-party and is only transferred to the seller's account after the buyer confirms on-time and satisfactory delivery of his order. This payment method is fairly safe for both the buyer and the supplier and is recommended for online purchases. Risk level: Low

Categories – This menu helps users further refine their search on Alibaba according to the category they are interested in. It is a great place to search for options if you have an idea of what you are looking for and the niche market you want to check but you do not actually have any specific product in mind.

Supplier information – On the right of the product page, there appears a small section that gives useful information about a supplier, which is important before a business decision is made. It tells the name of the supplier's company, whether the individual/company is verified, how long the individual/company has been in this business, how long they have been a Gold Supplier (if they are one), what their specialties and strengths are, what are the top markets they operate in and so on. All this information comes in handy when you want to understand if they are legitimate so you can gauge their authenticity.

Product Quick Details – When you scroll down the page, you can find some of the most crucial information about the product—material, size, color, etc. By switching from Product Details tab to Company profile, you can get all the information related to the company.

AliExpress – Alibaba has a sister website, AliExpress, which is an excellent marketplace for those who are looking for a targeted consumer market and not a business market. In the last couple of years, various e-commerce businesses have started getting their products sourced from AliExpress rather than Alibaba, particularly those who want products in smaller quantities. AliExpress ships most products for free to most regions across the globe, although the shipping time is up to 30 days.

Alibaba vs. AliExpress – Alibaba and AliExpress offer two different marketplaces that cater to different types of needs and, therefore, one might be a better choice for you over the other. While Alibaba is a marketplace that connects manufacturers and business owners and is perfect for those who are looking to place bulk orders at a lower price per unit, AliExpress is a marketplace that operates at a consumer level and allows business owners to buy products in smaller quantities at a factory price per unit. If you are looking to work directly with manufacturers and create your own products, or are looking for manufacturers who specialize in a certain kind of product which you can then private label under your own brand, Alibaba should be your pick. On Alibaba, you can work directly with a manufacturer, create your own private labeled product and place bulk orders. On the other hand, buying in bulk on AliExpress isn't a good plan as it is not considered as an effective way to buy stock for your business since the prices are comparatively higher than Alibaba. If you are someone who is looking for small MOQs, AliExpress should be your pick.

Buyer Beware!

Alibaba is great—no doubt about it. But, like any company, it does have certain issues that all the customers must be aware of before reaching out to suppliers. Here are some of the issues with sourcing suppliers:

• Middlemen: There are thousands of manufacturers who operate on this website, and not all are real. Some are just middlemen who tend to mark up the price of products and increase the level of confusion between buyers and sellers.

• Scammers who loot your money: Middlemen tend to increase the price, but they only take a bit of your money. Scammers do more damage. Although Alibaba has put together many policies to ensure you deal with only legitimate suppliers, there are still some dishonest suppliers who manage to break all the barriers and operate on Alibaba. So, you need to exercise caution, as on any platform.

• Quality is a subjective term: Although outsourcing overseas generally guarantees good quality, there are exceptions to every rule. Sometimes the product that sellers receive is not of high quality. Other times, there may be no intent to defraud, but your own definition of "high quality" might not match the manufacturer's.

These are a few things you can do to protect yourself and your money from bad manufacturers:

• Verification of suppliers – Alibaba has designed a program that includes multiple levels of verification – A&V Check, Supplier Assessment, On-site check and so on. All these checks have different badges that appear on supplier profiles and product listings as they are earned. Looking for these badges can be the first step in safeguarding yourself. There are also some third-party companies that offer to visit suppliers on your behalf to verify their identity and authenticity.

• Look for Gold Suppliers – All the manufacturers who are Gold Suppliers on Alibaba will bear a Gold Supplier badge on their profile/product page to let you know they have been given approval by Alibaba. They have also undergone and passed verification and authentication checks performed by third-parties. The badge provides information about the number of years a manufacturer has been active on Alibaba, which speaks to their trustworthiness and loyalty. Remember to run multiple filters as well as looking for the Gold Supplier badge.

• Follow up and ask questions – As you narrow down your options, ensure you ask for a manufacturer's contact details, business license and sample products. Set up a call and do some research about them online. Remember, you are not going overboard by doing all this. Do whatever it takes to make you more confident and comfortable in your business. You can even ask manufacturers to provide a couple of images of their workplace or someone holding one of their products.

• Ask for a sample product – Get samples to check quality before you spend a significant amount to have products made. You can even legally contact manufacturers using another email ID or account to get additional samples.

• Beware of the hidden costs (if any) – If you feel something is too good to be true, discuss the deal in detail and if you still feel something isn't right, just walk away from it.

• Look for the payment methods they accept – If a manufacturer accepts PayPal or the Secure Payment

System, it is a good sign for you as these are the two safest payment methods available. By using these services, you can make payment in installments, and you will not run the risk of paying for the entire amount upfront. These manufacturers might even offer dispute resolution services if one or both the parties fail to adhere to Alibaba's terms and conditions. Beware of the manufacturers who work only with the Western Union payment method as chances are high that there is a scam associated with them.

Contact Suppliers

Keep a spreadsheet of all potential suppliers that you feel are legitimate, including information such as Supplier name/link, FOB price, MOQ, Payment Terms, Gold Supplier-certified, Trade Assurance-certified and so on. This spreadsheet will help you have all the information available in one place so that you can always refer back to it.

When you are trying to contact manufacturers overseas, email is going to be your major source of communication. In most cases, particularly when you are dealing with manufacturers in non-English speaking countries, they use applications such as Google Translate to translate their email messages. To avoid misunderstandings, try to keep your email content simple, concise, spelling error free and well-formatted. This will help non-native speakers to better understand your message.

Another way to contact suppliers is to use Alibaba's instant messaging service. This instant messaging service connects with suppliers directly through their contact form, located at the bottom of the page. Clicking on Contact Supplier will take you to a different window where you can type your message and get connected.

Another means to connect with manufacturers is through Alibaba's TradeManager instant messaging service that provides you with a simple way to connect and manage your conversations.

Now that you are in touch with a reputable supplier, request a quote. Requesting a quote is quite simple on Alibaba and takes only a couple of minutes. Here are a few things you need to consider when requesting a quote:

• Look for MOQs – Though manufacturer might have listed a MOQ, ask again to ensure it is correct. If you feel the MOQ mentioned is high or unaffordable, provide an idea of what you can afford. Always bear in mind that MOQ is negotiable, particularly with suppliers overseas.

• Ask for sample prices – If you ask the manufacturer to send you a sample product so that you can check for quality, these samples might have an associated price and you should know about it before asking. Some manufacturers might charge the full retail amount to send you the sample, especially if they're getting too many requests. On the other hand, there are manufacturers who will offer a sample for free, or at least for a discounted price. So, instead of assuming things, ask any questions upfront.

• Know the production cost and time – More than the sample cost, it is the production cost that will make a difference in your buying decision. Ask your suppliers:

• How much will a unit cost?

• What is the price if you order in bulk?

• Are they open to negotiating the pricing?

• What is their production time?

• How long will it take to create a product once the order is placed?

• Ask about payment methods and terms – While some manufacturers let you pay them in installments, some accept orders only when paid upfront. So, understand the payment method and terms of the manufacturers clearly before you make your business decision. You can also ask about payment terms for future orders.

• Negotiate the terms and prices – You have been communicating with the manufacturer about payment methods and terms, production costs, etc. Now it's time to negotiate the MOQs, product cost and time.

• Ask about the logo and packing the product – Ask the manufacturer is if they will let you customize the package they provide and whether you can apply your brand logo to the product. If you are looking for private labeling for your product, you should be able to customize and add your brand to it so that it stands out among other similar products available in the marketplace.

• Ask about applying labels – Ask your manufacturer how they will deal with UPC labeling of the product. Will they apply it for you, or is this something you need to handle on your end? Each product needs to have a UPC before it is shipped to Amazon, so you must know if the manufacturer is applying it for you. If not, you will either have to get it done by a third-party agency or do it yourself. Remember that each product that goes through Amazon needs to have an FNSKU. You can ask your manufacturer to apply it for you; if not, Amazon will do it for an additional fee.

You now have all the details you need to place an order on Alibaba. Narrow down your options based on the information you have gathered such as price, MOQs, production time, payment terms and prices and the supplier's response time. If you find a deal that turns out to be too good to be true, be ready to walk away. Don't forget: there are hundreds of other options waiting for you.

If you don't hear back from a manufacturer, just remove them from your list. A supplier might not respond because:

• They're busy. A manufacturer's main job is to create products and manage tools/equipment/manpower to achieve that. Customer service or responding to disputes always takes a backseat. So, understand this well and keep sending follow-up messages. But if they take too long to respond, or do not respond at all, you need to move on and look for other options. Otherwise, you might face issues communicating with them later.

• The supplier might be on vacation. In this case, you can wait if you want to or move on to exploring the other options available.

• Your MOQ is too small. Sometimes suppliers do not show any interest if they see the MOQ is really small. They have defined MOQs for a reason and offering something that is too small can filter out your request. You can certainly propose something smaller than what they have quoted and then negotiate. Offering less, however, doesn't leave any scope for negotiations; suppliers may consider this a waste of time.

Next Steps After You Have Contacted Suppliers

Negotiation

It is fine to ask for a smaller MOQ. After all, manufacturers don't spend on buying raw materials, tools, labor, equipment each time they create products based on the effort required and size of the order. However, it will not be possible for them to produce your product for a price that is lower than the total expenses they will incur. Always consider these factors and negotiate with realistic figures. If you need a really small order, choose to go with AliExpress instead of Alibaba.

By negotiating, you are requesting that manufacturers do you a favor; you cannot, therefore, expect them to also slash their prices for you. While trying to meet your objectives, manufacturers might lower the quality of raw materials being used so that they can meet the lowered price while still making a profit. If you do not want to compromise on quality, be reasonable with the supplier and bear in mind that obtaining great quality might cost you a little extra.

There is a proper way to negotiate:

• Research as much as possible about your product including costs of raw material, production costs, production times, payment methods/ terms and shipping costs. This way you can measure the quote given by your supplier against what you already know to be true. You'll be able to judge if they have unreasonable demands on the quality, quantity and pricing.

• Be specific about details so that there is no chance of miscommunication. Be very clear about your questions and understand their responses so that neither party makes assumptions.

- If you are in touch with more than one supplier, you can perform a comparative analysis in order to make your business decision. This will enable you to determine which manufacturer is giving you a genuine quote and who is trying to take advantage of price, quality and quantity.

- Bring value to their business. You can do this by promising (and keeping your promise) that you will provide them with more clients, orders for more products and even offer them new gateways to explore new markets. This really works as the approach helps build a strong relationship between suppliers and customers.

- Be very calm and patient, but not beyond a certain limit that will affect your deadlines. Be vocal about your deadlines from the beginning and if you see your supplier will not be able to achieve the target within the defined timeframe, be ready to negotiate or move on.

- Third-party agencies and distributors mark up the product so that they can also make money. Therefore, make sure you are dealing with manufacturers directly, rather than middlemen.

- Document everything you agree on so that you can also refer to the document later in case of disagreements.

- Be professional and calm.

- Invest some time and resources if your supplier isn't taking you seriously. The main job of manufacturers is to create products and manage resources. Therefore, if they feel you aren't making inquiries with a real eye toward doing business, they will lose interest and won't waste their time on you.

- Walk away from the deal if you feel the manufacturer is trying to cheat you or is not giving you a good deal. They might come back to you later with a better price.

Commissioning a Product

If you are planning to sell something new and it doesn't already exist in the marketplace, you might need to do some research on the product before you look for someone to manufacture it for you. If your product is something similar to a product that is already on the top charts of Alibaba, you can contact suppliers who can make similar products with a modification or two. But if neither of these situations applies to your intended product, it means you are planning to sell something which is already in the marketplace (something similar), but are not able to choose which manufacturer to select. Then you can post a buying request on Alibaba. This way manufacturers will reach out to you, instead of you having to contact them.

When you have found a supplier who agrees to create your product within the defined timeline, send them the exact requirements of what you want in the product including the prototype, the wireframe, etc. If possible, send them a drawing or mockup sketch showing the exact product you need. Ensure you mention all dimensions, sizes, colors, etc. in detail; do not miss mentioning any important information as it might lead to confusion later. Give as many details as possible so that there is no room left for any issues. Be very specific about your plan and quantity so that the manufacturer is prepared for it.

Once you send all the details, along with the visual representation of how your product should look, ask for a few samples. When they send you the samples, evaluate them for quality and quantity. Conduct some tests on the product, such as a system test, drop test or whatever is appropriate to the product. The intent shouldn't be to find faults but to see if it fulfills your requirements and us durable. Send your feedback to the manufacturer and, if necessary, ask for more samples and repeat the same process until you get what you are looking for. You should not compromise on any requirements. Let them get the sample right before proceeding.

When you receive that perfect sample, place a small order and see if they can maintain a consistent quality with all products. Creating a sample might be easy, but it is important that they handle the mass production equally well. Discuss how they will handle any defective products—will they replace them or compensate you? Sometimes, particularly when the shipping cost is more, it doesn't make sense to send products back to the manufacturer. In such a case, most manufacturers either adjust the number in the next order or provide compensation.

If the small order goes smoothly and you are satisfied with what you receive, place a larger order.

What You Must Know Before Placing the Order.

While you are in the process of selecting a supplier, negotiating, receiving/ approving the samples and placing your first small order, there are certain things you must keep in mind.

• Are these products being sent to you or to the Amazon fulfillment center? If the products are being shipped to you directly, do you have enough space available to store them? If not, where will you store them?

• Have you taken into account the total costs of getting the products created? Is the number well within your budget? Has the manufacturer factored in the cost of tools and equipment required to create your products? What is the cost of one sample? What if you require more samples? Is all this within your budget? Be ready to see some additional costs and do not get carried away.

• Have you calculated your profit margins for selling this product? While calculating the profit, have you considered the cost of the product, assuming the quality remains consistent? Are you getting the right quality and quantity for the right price?

You must have a basic understanding of terms, such as intellectual property, copyrights, patents and trademarks.

- Trademarks – Protect the brand identity of an individual or business, such as brand names and logos

- Copyrights – Rights owned by a business or individual that protect the work such as content, photos, audios, videos, etc.

- Patents – Rights that protect ideas, such as creations, inventions, etc.

Generally, all these (copyrights, patents and trademarks) are not worthwhile as they are effective only in the country where you buy them. It's quite expensive to buy these rights and not worth it for beginners since they are just trying to develop their brand in the marketplace and likely don't have anything to protect yet. If something becomes popular and is liked by the customers on e-commerce sites such as Alibaba, others will copy that product or idea. If the manufacturers or other sellers see that something is successful, they will steal the product plan, information and pictures, and you are not protected and cannot stop it from happening. The best thing you can do to make your products and ideas stand out is to focus on your branding and marketing strategy to see how you can set your product apart from other products, whether it is in terms of price, quality or any another attribute. Beat the copycats with your innovative ideas, rather than legalities.

Establish Healthy Relationship with your Manufacturers

Your manufacturer is going to be akin to a business partner as their work will impact the success of your business. You are hugely dependent on them to give you the best possible product, and this forms the basis of your business. Therefore, always keep in mind that you need the support of your manufacturers more than anyone else. It is crucial that you establish a healthy relationship with your suppliers. Remember to:

• Always describe your requirements very clearly so that there is no room for any confusion. Be very specific about what you expect and how you want your product to be. It is always better to know things rather than assuming, so do not give them a reason to fail at meeting your expectations. They wouldn't want that either.

• Reciprocate well and on time. If you want them to respond to your queries and be available whenever you want, act the same way. After all, you get what you give. So, be there for them whenever they need something from you.

- Losing your patience can make things worse, so always be considerate and behave professionally, as a supplier might have different practices than what you follow in your country.

- Don't hesitate if you want to convey a message. It is always best to be upfront rather than facing issues later. If you do not want to be disturbed at any point, make it very clear that you are not available during that specific time. Tell them the best way to contact you, and ask them how they want to be contacted. This will make things simpler for both parties.

Shipping Information and Logistics

Shipping plays an important role in the buying process. Hence, you should know all the information and logistics about shipping before you place the order with the supplier. Remember that once shipped, products cannot be returned to the supplier, whether you like them or not. This is a no-return point. Before they ship the products to the defined destination, ensure you make two things very clear:

- Confirm and discuss their responsibilities – Reiterate their role and responsibilities in the invoice you are going to send them. Get confirmation of the cost of shipping products, agreed price of the products, the number of products that are being shipped and the expected delivery time

• Get proof of what they are sending – Before the product is shipped, ask for copies of the shipping label and photos/videos of the packaging and products.

Each supplier has their own options for shipping carriers, and you will have to select one of the options available. Each option will fall into one of these categories:

• Sea Freight (boat): The carrier ships by boat. If you opt for this method, remember that although it is the cheapest means of shipping, it takes the longest.

• Air Cargo (plane): The carrier ships by plane. If you opt for this method, although it is the quickest means, it will cost more. Also, not all products can be shipped by plane; for instance, some cosmetic products are considered hazardous. Make sure you research what products can and can't be shipped by air.

• Express (train): The carrier ships by Express, perfect for small orders.

Once you decide which method you want for shipping, work it out with the supplier and see what they can offer.

Sourcify to Source your Products

Sourcify is the platform that helps you bring your product idea to market. Sourcify understands how daunting it is to bring a product from your imagination to the real-life market if you have never done it before. You might have a great idea, an invention that can solve a problem, a product that can help millions or an improvised alternate option for something that already exists, but you don't know how to make it real. This is where Sourcify can help you. With a mission to bring your idea to life, it introduces business owners to the right supplier, helps you with the end-to-end product development process, walks you through the process of validating the legality of importing your item and allows you to make secure payments. This platform is based on a strong database that contains a comprehensive list of top-class sellers who are experts in a wide array of product manufacturing and design.

Get Started

To get started with Sourcify, join the platform, and you will be guided through each step of product development, whether you have the exact requirements of what you are looking for or just the idea. Whether you are a first-time seller or an individual/business owner who is looking to create products for better prices, Sourcify will connect you with some of the top manufacturers in the world.

The platform not only lets you source the products but also helps you sell them. And it's not just Sourcify—it's Sourcify + Shopify.

Even if you do not have any experience in coding or web designing, the platform lets you set up your online shop in a couple of minutes, list your items and start selling. You can also leverage its social marketing power to promote your product on various social handles, create followings and generate sales for your business.

Sourcify helps you evaluate the market for a product before you actually enter it. Use their dropshipping service, such as Oblero, an app that helps you import products that can be dropshipped directly into the Shopify store. Once you get an order from a customer, this product gets shipped to him/her directly. All you need to do is to keep a note of the difference in the amount you bought it for and the price you sold it for.

Canton Fair: Find the World's Best Manufacturers

Every year, hundreds of thousands of people from across the globe gather together at Canton Fair, the world's largest manufacturing tradeshow, to connect with top-class manufacturers so that they can design their business plan. Canton Fair brings together hundreds of trading companies, factories and business agents. The main reason several companies—of all sizes—come to this fair is that long-distance business relationships can break down any time, and dealing with your business partner in person can mark the beginning of a long-term relationship.

In order to attend the Canton Fair like an expert:

Do Your Homework: Research Before You Attend

If attendees do not have prior knowledge about their niche, they cannot take maximum advantage of the fair. Start researching manufacturers and potential industries online. Read about the manufacturers who are going to be present at the fair and see if you can match some of them to what you are planning to create. For example, if you are planning to sell yoga mats, search for manufacturers who offer this product. You can use the exhibitor product index to search for manufacturers.

Once you click on one of the listings from the search results, you can see details of the manufacturers, such as the name of the company/factory, the complete address, the booth number and the website link. Knowing the booth details in advance will save you time, as the fair is huge.

Socialize Before the Event: Get in touch with suppliers before you see them in person.

Try to connect with the manufacturers you are interested in working with as this gives you an advantage over others. When you look for details of manufacturers in the exhibitor product index, it gives you their email address and other contact information. Contacting them and creating a relationship before the event will give you a head start. You will feel connected when you meet them in person, and this will make the experience much better than meeting them as strangers.

Trade Show Tips:

Your main goal in visiting the fair is to find as many suppliers as possible (suppliers who can manufacture your product). With this aim in mind, doing a bit of research about who is coming to the event will help as will identifying the questions you want to ask these suppliers so that you can evaluate them and see who can do the best job for you. Some of these questions might be:

• Do you work as an individual or do you own a trading company? You should verify their answer by finding out the details at your end. You can browse the Internet or check the location provided by the index in Google maps to see if a factory exists or not. You can also read blogs in forums or other threads to see what is being said.

• In which country do you operate? Where do you send your products? This should give you an idea of the worth of the products. Some countries are very particular about what they want and expect to receive high-quality products.

• What kind of labels do you create? How about private labels? This is an important question if you are an FBA private label seller. Different suppliers have different requirements if you want them to private label the products for you. Some of them can only do it if you fulfill their Minimum Order Quantity, while others have a price per unit as the criteria. If it is about MOQ, you can negotiate with them by suggesting a slightly lower number. Tell them how it will help both you and them if you can agree on the suggested number, and how you can bring them more value and business.

- How much do you charge per unit? What are your production costs? Price shouldn't be the top priority for you when looking for a manufacturer. Ask for the price, but don't make your business decision based on their quote and don't spend too much time discussing the pricing factor as this might send the wrong message to the supplier.

Once you have your questions answered, prepare notes. The best thing is to create an Excel sheet with the names of different manufacturers you connected with/want to connect with. Create a column for each of the questions and answers. This will make the evaluation process easier as you will have all the details for all the manufacturers in one place. Have another column where you can mark the answer, and this column needs to be filled for each manufacturer once you speak to them. This step will help you analyze which suppliers you can follow up with after the event.

It is always a good idea to reach the venue early, when there are fewer competitors, so that manufacturers/sellers can focus on you more closely.

The Post Show

Now that you have a list of the shortlisted candidates, filter out all the "negatives" and the "maybes." Follow-up with all the "Yes" candidates post-event as soon as possible, as they might not remember you if you contact them a month later. Send follow-up emails to all the "Yes" suppliers by creating a common template and tweaking it for each of them. Just use the same template and change the supplier name. Here is an example of such an email

Dear name of supplier or individual,

My name is John Petersworth, and I met you last week during the Canton Fair. I really appreciate the time you invested in our conversation, and wanted to ask few more questions about your business.

- Can you private label your product for me?

- How much does your product cost per unit?

- What is the lead time?

It would be really great if you could help me with this information. You can reach me at XX@YY.com.

Also, could you please provide me a few alternatives of similar products that you have so I can analyze the details with my team? Thank you for your help, and I hope to hear from you soon. It is my hope that I will be placing an order with your company.

Thanks,

John

Sending a clear, concise email like this will help your supplier understand what you want, so there is a good chance that you will hear from them.

Attending trade fairs is an important step in growing your business because it is crucial that you find the best solution and best manufacturer to create your product.

Chapter 5: Branding on Amazon

While your first products are on their way to Amazon, it is a good idea for you to begin creating your brand. As you already know, your brand is key in helping you set yourself apart from other brands that already exist on Amazon. With your brand, you can create familiarity on Amazon itself, as well as on other platforms such as Instagram, Facebook, and Twitter, where you can drive traffic directly to your Amazon store.

If you chose to create private label products, you would want to have your brand already established before ordering them so that they are privately labeled with the right branding. For that reason, you should do this step before you officially purchase your products so that you can feel confident that they are going to match your branding.

In this chapter, we are going to explore all of the basics of launching a brand for your Amazon account, including how you can use other platforms to drive traffic to your website. You will also learn about how you can protect your brand to avoid having other Amazon merchants rip your brand off and potentially destroy your reputation and the credibility of your business along the way.

Choose Your Brand Identity

First things first, you need to choose your brand identity. Your brand identity is the identity by which you are going to be recognized, so you need to make sure that you choose one that is attractive and coherent. Your brand identity includes your name, your logo, your font, your colors, and your imagery. All of these factors are relevant in cultivating your brand, so make sure that you pay attention to all of them.

The name of your brand should be something relevant and catchy. It should make sense to your brand so that it is clear as to why you have chosen this name and what it represents. Ideally, your brand name should not be your own name, unless your own name is already popular and well known. Instead, choose a one or two-word brand name that represents what you are selling so that people will immediately recognize it and know who you are once you begin to establish brand familiarity.

Your logo and brand fonts should be the same, as you want to use your brand fonts in your logo. Typically, brands will choose two fonts that they are going to use to represent their brand. The first font is generally the header font that they are using, and the second font is the body font. These two fonts should go nicely together and should have a feel that is relevant to your industry. For example, if you are selling professional office products, you should use clean fonts like Arial or Helvetica. If you are in an elegant industry, choose something like a script header and a simple body font, such as Dancing Script and Arial.

You need to choose a few colors that are also going to represent your brand. Ideally, you should have three to four colors for your brand: one or two primary colors and then two secondary colors. Your colors are going to be used on everything from your labels to your graphics and everywhere else, so make sure they go well together and that they fit into your overall image. They should also be relevant to your industry by providing the right look and feel to your brand, as out-of-place colors can quickly make your brand seem unprofessional or misplaced.

Finally, you want to choose the actual imagery of your brand. Most brands will produce what is called a mood board, which is essentially a collection of graphics that give the feel for what your brand is going to offer. You might have people lying at the beach and sunsets if your brand is for lounging and relaxing, or you might have pictures of minimalism and fresh flowers if you want a minimalist eco-friendly appearance. Create whatever mood board you desire based on the look and feel that you want your brand to have.

Once you have put all of this together, lay it all next to each other to get a feel for what your final brand is going to be. This will give you an idea as to whether or not it works together and if it is going to provide the right look for your company. If you find that it does not perfectly reflect your brand, you are going to want to make a few adjustments to it so that it gives a better and more coherent feel for your customers.

Apply For Brand Registry

After you have created your brand, go on Amazon, and apply for a brand registry. You should do this before you do anything else with your brand as this is going to protect your brand from possible identity theft on Amazon. A brand registry can be applied for by going onto your professional seller account, heading to your settings, and selecting the "Brand Registry" feature.

In order to register your brand, you are going to have to provide the following information to Amazon:

- The name of your brand (it will need to be registered with U.S. Patent and Trademarks first)

- Brand serial number from your USPTO

- The countries where your products are manufactured and distributed by

- Image of your brand name on a product that you will be selling

- Image of your product label

- Image of your product

Although this can take some time, it is worth doing so that you can protect your brand from being stolen by anyone else on Amazon. Remember, Amazon is an international marketplace, so having this added layer of protection is crucial in helping you avoid any unwanted brand identity theft that could take place.

As well, having this brand registration unlocks more branded features for you on Amazon, including the ability to brand your own storefront and product pages as per your brand's appearance. It is well worth the investment!

Brand Your Product Pages

Each time you upload products to your shop, you should be branding those pages. There are three areas of your product page that you want to brand in order to have your brand clearly displayed for your customers to see.

The first part of your product page you want to brand is your title. Your title can have up to 200 characters in it, so do your best to create a full title that features your brand's name, the title of the product, and anything else that someone may search when they are looking for your products.

The second part of your product page that you should brand is your product description. On Amazon's product pages, you can include up to 5 bullet points of information, with each bullet point containing up to 255 characters. Use these bullet points to provide clear information about what benefits people will gain from using the products and any search terms that they may be looking for when they are searching for products like yours. Refrain from making the bullet points spammy by listing search terms without any context, as this may actually reduce your rankings on Amazon's SEO, or search engine returns.

Finally, you want to brand your pictures. Your pictures should clearly display your product with your branded private label. You can also watermark your images with your brand name in the corner or somewhere along the edges, where it will not interrupt your image so that you can brand your product there as well. Each of your pictures should be relevant to your brand by having your brand's color scheme and mood artistically weaved into your picture. For example, if you have a fresh and clean eco-brand, you might photograph your product on a white background next to fresh green plants. If you have a rustic western brand, you might photograph your product on a wood background next to something like a vintage piece of furniture or decoration. Avoid going too crazy with your images; however, as cluttered images or images with too many decorations in them can be distracting and confusing. People may get overwhelmed with what they are looking at and may find themselves looking elsewhere instead of looking at your products because they simply do not know what they are looking at.

Brand Your Product Labels

In addition to branding your store, you also want to brand your product labels. Whenever you can, source products that allow for private labels so that you can label your products with your logo, fonts, and color scheme. Doing so is going to help you create products that are marketing your brand for you as they feature all of this information directly on them. Now, when someone buys your product, they are going to remember the brand it was purchased from, and they can use this information to buy more for themselves or to encourage their friends to buy something from you.

When you brand your product labels, try to stick to generally the same look on all products. Having the same background colors, imagery, and general design on your product labels will ensure that you are keeping your look uniform. This way, you are increasing your chances of having brand recognition because you are producing the same look every time. A great example of this is Coca-Cola. Their brand is represented by an iconic red with their scripted logo. Every time you look at a Coca-Cola product, you immediately know what it is because the branding is uniform and clear every single time.

Brand Your Amazon Storefront

On Amazon, after you register your brand, you are going to have the opportunity to brand your storefront.

Your storefront is basically like your webstore or your own private webpage on Amazon's platform that displays your products for sale. Branding your storefront is an important part of making it memorable so that people want to see it and pay attention to your products when they land on your page.

You can brand your storefront by choosing how many pages you are going to have displayed on your store, what those pages are, and what categories they revolve around. You want to design your pages and categories in a way that reinforces the image and brand that you have already begun to develop so that when people land on your page, it feels like it truly belongs to your brand. In other words, it makes sense.

When you develop your storefront, a branded video on your front page that is about 30 seconds long is actually an incredible way for you to boost your viewership and your recognition. Although this will take more effort and time investment on your end, doing it can have a huge impact on your customers and can support you with increasing your sales numbers.

With your branded storefront, you can choose to have your own URL if you desire so that you can market both on Amazon's platform and off of it. If you really want to set yourself apart from the other brands on Amazon, this is a great feature. However, it is not necessary, so do not feel like you have to do this if you do not want to. You can still make plenty of money with your Amazon FBA platform without your own URL.

Brand Your Amazon Ads

Amazon offers three types of ads: sponsored product ads, sponsored brand ads, and sponsored display ads. Taking advantage of sponsored brand ads is a great way to promote your brand and help boost brand recognition so that you are more likely to make sales with your brand on Amazon. As well, sponsored brand ads provide you with the opportunity to show people what your brand is so that they can find your store and discover what products they are interested in, rather than having your individual products being marketed to them.

Brand Your Other Platforms

Once your Amazon brand has been built, brand your other platforms, too. With Amazon, you are not required to use social media to drive traffic to your store. However, it does help. Driving your own traffic to your own store by building a brand on social media and using that brand to funnel people increases your sales because it means you are no longer relying solely on Amazon's algorithm. You certainly do not have to do this, and if you do not want much involvement in this business you should skip this step, but if you really want to grow your store, this is an important step.

If you are on Instagram, Facebook, Twitter, or anywhere else on social media or the internet itself, make sure that you are branding your accounts. Use your logo in your graphics, choose graphics that are relevant to your brand, and create a brand that is going to help you establish recognition. Then, encourage people from your brand to find their way to your platform and purchase your products!

There are plenty of great books about branding on social media, so I highly recommend you grab one and use that as a part of your mindset growth and personal development if this is something you want to do. A book that is specifically designed around this topic will provide you with ample advice on how to brand each account and how to post in a way that accentuates your brand and gets your name out there in a bigger way.

Chapter 6: Amazon Tools for Getting Started

There are many tools that you will need to get started with selling on Amazon. In this chapter, you will find a list of essential tools that will help you in starting out as a seller on Amazon.

Freightos:

Every part of the selling machinery on Amazon is automated, except the part where a salesperson will have to import their goods to the Amazon warehouse(s). Dealing and coordinating with freight movers can be a time-consuming process, and you will never know if you are getting a good deal or not. Freightos offers an international freight calculator, letting you compare the freight prices of air, water and trucking costs in an instant. Not just that, but you can also compare the prices of different logistics providers as well. This will help to ensure that you are getting the best available price on your freight charges.

Sellics:

Everything that you will require to start selling on Amazon is made available in one place with Sellics.

There are seven different features that this tool offers. The most attractive features offered by it include keyword ranking, inventory management, and profit calculation. You can categorize and analyze the benefits at the SKU level as well as by organic or PPC sales. Profit calculation is quite detailed, and it includes several filters like the cost of goods sold, costs of inbound shipping, and much more.

JoeLister:

This is perhaps the quickest way an Amazon seller can list their inventory—not just on Amazon, but on eBay as well. It will save you lots of time and effort by creating an inventory listing for Amazon. It only takes a few clicks, and this application will make sure that your item quantities are synced so that you don't oversell. Whenever a sale is made, this application will create a multichannel fulfillment order on Amazon along with the tracking information. And you, as a seller, won't have to do anything. It will also help you to make decisions regarding pricing and help the buyers leave an automatic feedback as well. What's more? You can take advantage of this service for free for two weeks. If you feel that it will be beneficial, then you can subscribe to it.

Forward2me:

This application provides a service for managing returns, and it offers two essential services. It provides customer returns and the return of excess stock. According to Amazon guidelines, sellers will have to provide a local address for receiving the returns, or they have to pay for return orders or return shipping on all the returns. For a retailer selling from a foreign location, this can be an expensive process. This application provides a very simple solution to manage this issue and reduce the overall costs. You can also make use of this application to make sure that the excess stock or inventory is returned from Amazon's warehouse to your location. You need to provide Forward2me with your forwarding address, and this application will do the rest. The sign-up process is quite simple as well.

Amazon Seller App:

If you are interested in retail arbitrage, then this is a great application for scanning products that you have come across and you think might have the potential to be sold on Amazon FBA. What's more? This application is free of cost. You can try out Amazon FBA without spending too much on acquiring inventory. It also allows a seller to list particular items available for sale, contact Amazon, and respond to customer inquiries. It allows you to check the current rates, sales ranking, and customer feedback by using the text-based search option.

Inventory Lab:

Inventory Lab, as the name suggests, allows a seller to manage not just their inventory but their accounting as well. This application allows sellers to check their profitability and keep an inventory of their stock in real-time. You can even print labels directly through this application. The elegant yet robust accounting provisions of this application will help you keep track of all your business expenditure.

Scoutify:

Inventory Lab developed this app, and it allows sellers to explore multiple competitive deals on Amazon through their phone. The user interface is very easy, and it offers a lot of helpful features. This application comes with Bluetooth scanner compatibility; a seller can see the gross profit of each product, weigh in the costs for the calculation of net profit, review their search history and monitor any decline in earnings, estimate the taxes to be paid, and so on.

Camelcamelcamel:

If you want to consider FBA as a seller, then this is one of the most useful tools available, and it is free. This helps to monitor the price listings of products on Amazon, keeps track of the sales, and much more. This application includes a browser add-on, provides you with Amazon's price charts, and also tracks the price changes as well. This application enables you to set up alerts for price and availability, whenever there are any changes. Prices of listings will constantly be updated from Amazon to make the data as reliable as possible.

Profit Bandit:

This isn't a free application, but the price you pay for it is quite reasonable. It offers services like a built-in filter that automatically shows the profit or loss on individual products. It also has the option to display collectibles, and you are allowed to research within this platform before deciding on your sales by checking other websites.

Price Blink:

This application is a software add-on, and it provides you with details about items that are offered for a lower price on other websites. If you are looking to sell a particular product through Amazon, then you can make use of this application to check if the same is being offered for a lower price on other websites. This comes in handy if you are leaning towards retail arbitrage. This platform can be easily accessed and is quite unobtrusive. When you click on a particular listing on this portal, it will check the web and show you the results. You can compare the prices and price your products accordingly.

Pickasin:

ASIN stands for Amazon Standard Identification Numbers, and these are used to identify items on Amazon. It consists of 10 letters or numbers, or a combination of these two, for searching items provided in the Amazon catalog. If the item is listed on Amazon, it will appear in your search results. If you are interested in selling on Amazon, then you should have a tool that will allow you to select ASINs easily, and this free tool helps you to do just this.

Shipping boxes:

If you are just starting, then you can collect shipping boxes from different places like your local stores or even Craigslist. It is essential that you pick up some shipping boxes if you want to start selling your products on Amazon. Pack your products in shipping boxes and ship them to the Amazon warehouse. Depending on the size of the items you have listed for sale, you can select the size of your shipping boxes as well.

Shipping scale:

You will need to check the weight of the package before you ship it. It is important to weigh a package because depending upon the weight of a package, the shipping charges might vary.

USB Barcode scanner:

Listing items does get easier when you don't have to enter the UPC of every listed item into Amazon manually. If you are dealing with a large number of items, then this tool will help you save time and money as well. You don't have to install software, and it is quite easy to use. This scanner is a good investment, and it will certainly come in handy.

Purchase a label printer, poly bags, packing tape and glue before you start selling your products on Amazon.

Chapter 7: Create a strong customer experience

Providing great customer service is a major way that you can compete with other sellers and win repeat purchases. Prompt shipping and communication are the pillars of providing great service and greatly influence your feedback from customers. Amazon says that when sellers respond to a customer's order inquiries, they receive only half as much negative feedback as customers who take more than 24 hours to respond.

One of the primary ways you'll interact with buyers is through Amazon's seller message service. To access it, click on the Messages link at the top right corner of Seller Central.

Amazon keeps tabs on your contact response time. You can check your metrics by hovering over the Performance tab in Seller Central and selecting Account Health from the drop-down menu. Then select the Performance Metrics tab. Along with your contact response time, you'll see metrics on your order defect rate, cancellation rate, late shipment rate, and several other items.

Managing customer feedback

Customers can leave feedback on your seller account to evaluate their shopping experience. Monitoring your feedback is a must—you want to build a track record of providing a great customer experience and of knowing that buyers are happy with the products you're selling. A summary of your feedback accompanies all your product listings on Amazon detail pages and can greatly influence buyer decisions. A seller with a stellar feedback average can charge a premium over sellers with spotty feedback.

View your feedback by hovering over the Performance tab at Seller Central, then select Feedback from the drop-down menu.

You'll be transferred to the Feedback Manager page, where you can view short- and long-term metrics. You can click on the Order ID to view transaction details and view an encoded version of your buyer's e-mail address in case you need to contact them.

If you see a one-star or two-star review, click the Resolve button to contact the customer. Perhaps the customer's order delivery took longer than expected.

You might refund their shipping fee as a goodwill gesture. And in return, you can ask the customer to modify or remove their negative feedback from your account. Here are the instructions for removing feedback that you can pass along to your buyer:

Go to Your Submitted Feedback at https://www.amazon.com/gp/feedback/view-all-feedback.html

Click Remove link next to the feedback you would like to remove.

Be sure not to pressure or coerce the buyer, as this tactic may backfire and it's a violation of Amazon policy.

In some cases, a buyer who left negative feedback won't respond. In that case, you can use the Respond button to post a message to rebut the negative feedback, explaining how you worked to resolve the problem. It won't change your feedback score, but other customers who review your feedback in the future may be reassured by your explanation.

Buyers are able to edit or delete their feedback during a 60-day window, after that, the feedback cannot be changed. Generally, Amazon will not get involved in a dispute over feedback. But occasionally Amazon will remove buyer feedback if it meets these conditions:

- Includes obscene language

- Includes personal information

- The entire review is a product review, not a review of the buying experience

- A complaint about fulfillment or customer service on an FBA order

Customer satisfaction reports

Access your Customer Satisfaction Reports by hovering over the Performance tab at Seller Central and select Account Health from the drop-down menu. Hover over the Reports tab, and you'll see links to the three reports Amazon provides to help you gauge your customers' satisfaction:

1. Order Quality Report: Shows the points you received from each of your orders. The points are used to calculate your seller rating. When you click through to the report, you'll see a list of recent orders accompanied by the points earned. You'll see the

specific issues with orders (late shipment or negative feedback, for example).

2. Performance over Time: Shows some of your key account health metrics. You can filter the report by a specific time period or certain product lines.

3. Performance by Product Line: Breaks down order errors by category. You'll see which product categories generate the most problems.

Managing returns and chargebacks

No matter how great your products are or how superb your order fulfillment was, you'll get a steady drip-drip of returns. It's just a cost of doing business that is beyond your control, and the best attitude to have is to graciously accept returns and give buyers the benefit of the doubt.

At the bare minimum, you're required to meet Amazon's written return policy, which is to accept returns within 30 days of the customer receiving your shipment. Some products have different policies or requirements.

When you receive a return request, you'll receive an e-mail that includes the buyer's reason for submitting the request. (Of course, this applies to seller-fulfilled transactions only—FBA returns are handled by Amazon, and if you receive an inquiry from an FBA customer regarding a return, you can politely refer them to Amazon's staff.)

You should respond to the return request within 24 hours and indicate whether you will accept or decline the return. To reply to a request, hover over the Orders tab at Seller Central and select Manage Returns from the drop-down menu. On this page, you can authorize a return request, issue a refund, or contact the buyer. You may close the request if you don't plan to authorize the return, or you don't require the item to be returned in order to issue a refund.

If you require the buyer to return the item, you should wait until you receive it before issuing a refund. You'll want to inspect the item to ensure it remains in good condition.

Once you authorize a return, you can upload a customer return label. This enables you to authorize prepaid return shipping.

You can outline your return policies in Seller Central. Hover over the Settings tab at the top right corner, and select Return Settings from the drop-down menu. Enter your return instructions into the text box and click Save Settings. Also on this page you can choose whether you want Amazon to automatically authorize all return requests, or you want to authorize them yourself on a case-by-case basis.

Chapter 8: Leverage your descriptions

For your product listing, it's time to determine what your customer wishes to see when they have located your product, and to also decide how you are going to market your product to them.

One of the main elements is choosing optimized keywords in describing your products, and you'll see how these keywords do most of their work in the background. Another crucial factor is to use the same keywords your competitors are using, so we will also look at how you can achieve that too.

Another section of the product page is what customers will see, this is your title, description, and any bullet points. Here, you need to be descriptive without being overly technical, and above all, you need to keep an element of being personal with your customer. Being human in your description is far better than appearing like a company who doesn't care much.

Reviews and a keen price are other areas in which we'll delve into a little later on.

Optimizing Your Keywords

At the time of choosing keywords, you need to draw customers in, the ones who are looking for your products. This leads to higher conversion rates, and remember, your conversion rates are determined by how many people buy your product after viewing it. It's no use having lots of views if nobody buys your product.

Consider a product in a niche. As an example, we'll use a blanket with a picture of a baby playing with a dog; you might have to optimize keywords for "blanket" and "baby." Most people who are looking for blankets will need something which is much more understandable. "Blanket" alone is nowhere near enough to make your blanket stand out from plain blankets.

Additionally, people might not be looking for a minor aspect of the product. If they search for "baby" and "blanket," they're more than looking for an actual baby. They might, however, be looking for a baby blanket, so it's important to optimize the word "baby" as a keyword here. There's no point in attracting one type of customer with basic keywords when they need another other product, so make sure you add the secondary keywords to differentiate your product from others.

To put it all in a summary, you don't merely need the highest number of views as possible, what you need is as many views as possible from customers who will want to buy your product. So, all real keyword optimization allows for is: as much as weeding out people who don't want your product, it also continues attracting people who do want it. The best of both worlds!

Chapter 9: How to launch a new product on Amazon

Now that you have a solid idea of how the process of private labelling works from a broad perspective, let's take deeper look at some of the essential elements of this type of business. Finding the exact right types of products on which to ultimately base your private labels is the absolute lifeblood an Amazon private label business. If you were to have a great "mechanical" organization to your business (efficient SEO, streamlined reports, responsive inventory management, etc.), but select the wrong products, it would be similar to having a fancy Corvette with new tires and shiny paint but a weak engine. One undoubtedly needs tires and seat to drive a car, but once these aspects are in place, the engine is the most important factor that makes the car run well or not.

Product selection is by far the most "artful" aspect of the process and it has the most considerations. By "artful" I do not mean that this part of the process relies on intuition over numbers or observed results. I mean that unlike configuring your Amazon account, this is not a process that can be fully described in an exact "A,B,C,D..." format. Being successful in product selection requires thinking conceptually as well as finding which sort of approach suits your own strengths and tastes.

A great place to start would be looking at and evaluating the general approach taken by Will Tjernland../../../Downloads/h - footnote33, one of the most successful practitioners of private labeling through Amazon. These are not hard and fast rules, but rather examples of a great way to think about the process. Your approach will likely differ somewhat.

Will looks for three general qualities when considering a product:

1) The product is a good size

2) Has minimal electronics

3) Is not a product that people exclusively buy the brand name

His reason for favoring heavier products relates to the free two day shipping incentive of Amazon Prime. There exists even more incentive to purchase through Prime if you are buying something of a higher weight (since shipping costs would be much higher if you had to foot the bill yourself). However, since he is shipping a mass order to Amazon in one shot (the initial wholesale order from the supplier), shipping charges are relatively small on a per unit basis. Furthermore, he figures that there will generally be less competition on heavier items.

The reason for favoring products with no or little electronics is simple: fewer things that can break and therefore fewer returns and negative reviews.

Reason three is essential -- it is likely very difficult to compete in a space where people almost exclusively trust brand name products. Even if a cheaper alternative is indeed viable, there exist intangible reasons why customers will still prefer purchasing brand name products. For example, take the example of golf equipment - would creating a private label for golf equipment work? Take a moment to brainstorm "why" or "why not."

A fairly precise answer to this question would be as follows: for the most part, golf equipment would be a poor candidate for selling as a private label product, but it depends on what type of golf equipment is in question. Clubs and balls would likely not be successful as the vast majority of customers who depend on time tested brands -- almost to the point of superstition. "I've been using Titleist golf balls since age ten and never plan to change." Accessories such as golf umbrellas, towels, or tees have potential, but one would need to consider margins. If the item is too inexpensive, it may be tough to make a profit after Amazon's fulfillment fees.

Conversely, something like a door weatherstrip might make an excellent private label product. Brand-wise, it would be hard to imagine anyone caring in the least who is the maker of product. Does it insulate the house from drafts or does it not?

The most important question to ask when searching for products is "how or why would a product I list gain an advantage over or gain a share along with existing products sold?" The more competitive the market, the less likely it is to be that you will be able to add value and compete. For example, if there is a gas station on every corner in your town, it probably does not make sense to open one right in between two existing ones (unless you can somehow provide a reason to make buying gas at your store better -- perhaps an attached convenience store with better food).

There are other examples besides price, where you may be able to gain an advantage (however if you do find a way to bring a quality product to the market at a better price, you may not need other advantages). For example, maybe there is a way to bundle related products in a convenient way for buyers. Or perhaps there is a niche where few products are listed on prime. Moreover, you might find a selection of products with unclear listings, poor pictures, and low response rates to questions. Bring a product to market where you do all of these things better and provide a product of exactly equal quality could be enough to gain the upper hand in that market over time. An alternate way to think about this same concept would be to take the listing and ongoing metrics outlined in the Amazon SEO and evaluate how well existing listings are satisfying these metrics and if there is room for improvement.

Product ideas can come from anywhere -- such as in our hypothetical example of selling private label lawn furniture. When considering if private labeling is the right business for you, you would be well advised to start cultivating the habit of being aware of the products you use or buy on a day to day basis, looking them up, and comparing them on Amazon. Click through the related links, categories, and subcategories to get a feel an overall feel of the various markets. Sometimes an idea might come first (like with the lawn furniture) and the tool will be useful in drilling down on this idea. For example, once you become interested in lawn furniture you could use tools to run an analysis on the actual sales volume of all similar items. In some cases, using a tool might actually be the genesis of your idea, pulling you towards potentially profitable product categories at which you might not have foreseen looking.

Trying to understand the demand in a market is just as important as evaluating the supply (existing competitor listings). Demand can be estimated at several stages. First, using tools it is possible to extract data (timing of sales, prices, total revenue). Upfront analysis can be an effective way to compare markets on a relative basis. Another way to assess demand is the selling of your sample order. However, some creative sellers (Will Tjernland in this case) are taking steps to further evaluate demand in between these two stages by selling a few units they have not bothered to actually hold. Once the units sell, they fulfill the order from another listing or buy the unit from a wholesaler and have it shipped directly to their address. Using this technique, units are sold at a slight overall loss, but this slight loss is considered an investment in information in the market (and much cheaper than making a full order).

As with any FBA related objective outlined in this book (or elsewhere), the key is to have the hunger to learn the different alternatives available for accomplishing that objective, experiment with the ones that seem promising, and determine which techniques are most suited to your particular style. For example, a seller might be a lifelong shopper who has many years of experience buying household goods for his family. Perhaps because of his tangible experience with products he is able to find niches on Amazon by more of an intuitive method -- just knowing "what people like" and at what price it will sell. Another FBA seller might be a recent graduate who does not have much experience with products but is a wizard analyzing data and trends. Both intuitive and quantitative approaches to product selection can be successful. As with any business, experimentation and trial and error are necessary. Your own approach will be crafted over time.

Reviews Are Extremely Important

One of the most influential factors when it comes to sales are the reviews. If optimizing and advertising play a decisive role in making the product more visible and boosting the rankings, reviews are responsible for increasing the conversion rate. Shoppers are constantly looking for information regarding a merchandise, after all. Having a well-structured product description is a big plus because the buyers can find important details related to the goods, such as specifications and a nicely written description. If you can write it as a story, that is a bigger bonus. What they also want to find is the opinion of other buyers regarding your product. The reviews are valid social statements connected to your merchandise; in many cases, the shoppers consider them the most trustworthy. A few things that you can see in a customer's feedback are:

- user experience

- shipping

- quality of the product

The specialist reviewers like to write them as a list of advantages and disadvantages. They usually cover the points mentioned above, primarily if the product is user-friendly and it meets the customer's expectation related to quality and design, along with the delivery process itself. As users pop on this platform with a clear intention to buy products, the reviews are most influential when taking the decision to buy a product, assuming that the description and specifications already meet the buyer requirements. The more feedback you get, the more likely your product will sell. The A9 algorithm sees the reviews as extremely important, and it indexes them accordingly. As soon as you get your first review, this will mean an impressive boost in rankings. If you conduct your business in a niche with less competition, around ten to 20 sales should guarantee a spot for your product in the first two pages. Some merchants realized the importance of the reviews and tried to obtain them "artificially" by paying individuals to write reviews of products. This practice is not accepted by Amazon because it creates a fake image of a merchandise in front of customers. They have extremely strict terms and conditions related to this practice, but you can still find some tools to get honest reviews. Customers come first in Amazon's view; that's why they are focusing on achieving their satisfaction and protecting them from products of poor quality. If shoppers always consult the reviews when buying a merchandise online, merchants should also do that to improve the quality of their products and services. By listening to your customers (and consumers of your competitors), you can adjust and customize your products and services according to the needs of your customers. Sales may win you some people once, but the customer service and the quality of your product will give you their absolute loyalty. If you consider Amazon Retail, most of their consumers only use this platform to buy a broad range of products. They do not need to look anywhere else because they are extremely satisfied with the services and products provided by Amazon. At a lower scale, this is what you need to aim for. Furthermore, respecting the "voice" of your customers expressed through the reviews can undoubtedly help you achieve this objective.

Find Something to Boost Your Initial Sales

Let's consider that you are completely new to Amazon and want to make good money by selling high-quality goods to different buyers. At this point, you have the listings prepared, your content is optimized with keywords used in a natural manner, and you have very artistic photos well-structured and informative product description. However, you are still missing that special something to trigger your first sales. You know that you will be charged anyway by Amazon for your inventory, regardless if you make sales or not. As you are on this platform to sell goods, you can't afford to lose time so you need sales to start kicking immediately. In order to achieve this objective, besides optimizing your content, you will need to consider using Amazon Advertising to generate your first sales, particularly the Sponsored Products ads campaign. This involves setting buying special spots, which are extremely visible on the first page of results. It's also called Amazon PPC because you will place your product in that special spot, and you will pay for each click being made on your product. Since users are most likely interested to buy, they don't fool around when clicking on such an advertisement. If they like what they see, they will definitely buy a product. You need to set up your daily budget as well, which will cover a limited amount of clicks. This tool is your best chance of getting your first sales, making your first money on Amazon, and starting your journey to the top of the rankings.

Amazon Coupons

It's really hard to refuse a product that comes with a discount, especially when you are already interested in it or it is similar to the items that you are into. An interesting sale strategy is to have the first products sold for a lesser price to attract more shoppers towards your product. Of course, you merely can't sell all your existent inventory at a reduced rate; that's why it's important to set a limited amount of items that you want to sell for a discount. This a good way to make potential customers aware of your brand's merchandise. Traffic on Amazon can also be generated by external sources, such as your social media or business website. You can post an ad on Facebook or send customized emails to your customers from the database that you already have to announce your presence on Amazon and give them special offers. You can sweeten the deal by throwing in an Amazon coupon that's designated to provide a discount on one of your listed products on the platform. If you are hoping to get your first sales using this process, and let's say you have a few Amazon Coupons to give away, then you need to work intensively on this marketing campaign. After all, your presentation will need to reach more and more potential customers to become very effective. It's only up to you to choose your default sales trigger - whether you want to advertise through social media, send plenty of emails to your existing customers, give away discount coupons or choose the Amazon PPC option. Advertising on the platform can reach a higher number of customers compared to using external sources and offering coupons.

Follow Up to Get a Feedback

The most effective sale is the one that generates feedback because it creates all the necessary conditions to climb up on rankings, increase product visibility, and eventually generate other sales. In the old days of trade, sales were done through recommendations as well. The "word of mouth" was spread, and more and more people were aware of a specific product and its advantages. Sales triggered other sales, in other words. Things are about the same when it comes to online selling platforms, considering reviews and feedback are proven methods to produce more sales. The ideal situation is to get either after every sale, but it is genuinely hard to think of a seller which has achieved this performance. Reviews and feedback boost the popularity of the product and brand awareness, and shoppers are most likely to buy famed items because they are already considered trustworthy. A piece of good advice is to follow up with the customer to find out what he or she thinks about the merchandise. In the eyes of the shoppers, after all, it proves that you care about them and that you are willing to go the extra mile to satisfy their needs. This is the way to get positive feedback and reviews, which is something that Amazon and the users that are present on this platform appreciate very much. Another good idea is to comment on a customer review directly, thanking them for their opinion.

Chapter 10: How growing your sales

Some minor success should fuel the fire, but that means a lot of hard work is ahead if your FBA business is going to be more than a mild success. There is no get-rich-quick method. You may have a wildly successful month, but you are still going to have to work hard to make sure the next month is also wildly successful, at least until you're established. Here are some of the secrets to helping you work ON your business instead of working FOR your business.

Don't Burn Out on Retail Arbitrage

The major problem most entrepreneurs face when trying to scale up their Amazon FBA business is the deadly burnout that makes them not want to ever step foot in a store or list another item on Amazon again. This happens when we hit the ground running too hard and sell too many one-off products.

If you love shopping, you may never burn out on that particular process. If you don't mind typing up condition notes while you watch TV, then you are a true warrior. However, that only goes so far. There are only so many days in a week, so many hours in a day, and at some point you simply aren't going to be able to scale any further if everything you sell is sold in quantities of one. If you keep trying to go this route, you almost inevitably burn out without seeing a huge increase in profits. Even if you don't quit, that's called "maintaining," and that's probably not your goal.

At this stage, you're almost your own employee instead of being your own boss. There are a ton of perks to retail arbitrage, but it isn't the end-all be-all for everyone making a living on Amazon FBA. Of course, some people stick to this method and do well.

Move Into Wholesale

One of the huge perks of starting off with retail arbitrage is that you have the opportunity to learn about a lot of different categories and products. If you take the time to review your sales and understand what seems to sell easily and what doesn't, what is easy to find cheap but sells high, then it goes to reason that you can take that knowledge and extend it into wholesale.

The perks of wholesale are plentiful. Not only are you getting the best possible deal for the products you're going to sell, but you also eliminate the constant pricing and scanning of new products. Instead of writing condition notes for 100-500 separate items— burn out imminent!—you can buy in bulk, write a single condition note for the product, set a single price, and ship them with identical labels. This cuts down on the workload and frees you up to continue scaling your business.

Finding that great wholesale product (and then the next great wholesale product) is hard work, but the payoff becomes an inventory that doesn't require a huge amount of time cleaning, prepping, and preparing several items from different categories.

Move Into Private Label

We've discussed private label in great detail in the sourcing products chapter, and while the risks can be high, the same truths apply to private label as wholesale: once you find a great product, the rest of the work with listing is only done a single time. While you will have to develop content, you can outsource some of the work involved in making sales copy convincing and powerful, utilizing great minds to help sell your product. The workload becomes marketing and branding centric instead of hitting the pavement.

The great thing about private label is that you can truly focus on what you love. You can create a community and brand around a hobby or interest you have, and in doing so, the work becomes more enjoyable than trying to sell every single thing under the sun. This one seems very obvious, but it is often overlooked by those tackling the beginner's mentality of going out and finding products to sell. The more you love a product, or the lifestyle around it, the better you will be able to connect with your potential customer in your marketing efforts through your website, blog, social media, etc.

Scaling private label once you have a few successful products becomes easier. As a brand gains recognition for quality and good customer support, putting out new products that reach your market base is going to be the easiest method to continue scaling. There's no reason a successful brand couldn't put out new products several times a year. There's a lot of work involved for each one, but as you grow, affording the help from freelancers becomes less and less of a burden.

Advertise

This works best with private label sales, but it also moves into wholesale and larger distribution models. In the event that you have chosen to specialize in a certain category, it is time to build your platform with that blog, website, social media, and... paid ads!

While this method may not be practical for every solution, paid advertisements through Facebook, Adsense, and Bing Ads are proven to drive large amounts of traffic. With a private label item, some forms of advertising are essential to your success.

The trick about advertising is that it requires testing. Lots of testing. Always create at least two ads for every product you intend to advertise. Test these ads against each other, scrap the one that doesn't work as well, and build a new one to pit against the other. Dig deep for keywords that are under-utilized by sellers in the same category, and test some more.

If marketing really isn't for you, this process can be outsourced to some extent, but keep in mind that more people touching your business, the more costs involved. In an ideal scenario the rise in profits will justify this, but there is some risk involved.

Learning how to advertise is a huge job unto itself, but taking advantage of the information you have from your reports will help targeting your market a little bit easier.

Improve the Quality of Your Listings

It cannot be stressed that a high-quality listing, especially for private label items or any items where you've created the product page, is going to have a huge impact on the amount of sales you are able to make. If your content is not professional, buyers will write your products off more often than not. By improving the quality of your listings with better condition notes, including images, and writing descriptions for those products you're branding yourself or created a listing for, you're putting professionalism first, and that is not lost on the customer (even if they don't realize it).

Seek Out Reviews

Again, this applies mostly to those with private label products or those that have created product listings for items that are otherwise not available on Amazon. With positive customer reviews comes more customers. It's a proven fact that people respect the word of actual purchasers.

To facilitate an increase in reviews, you will need a method of contacting people that are likely within the market your products land in. If you are private label selling, then you should be developing an online presence, and through this you can offer an item for free in exchange for a review on Amazon. Note that you cannot ask for a positive review; you can simply ask them to give their honest opinion. For this reason, and so many others, you need to make sure that you only sell durable and useful goods.

This method has done a lot for me. Through one of my email lists, I invited people to claim free gifts in exchange for a review on Amazon, a video unboxing, or some other form of honest feedback (and promotion) for the item. All they had to do was send me some proof of their contribution, and they were guaranteed first dibs on the next round of freebies as well. This garnered roughly 20 reviews on Amazon and a few video unboxings on somewhat popular YouTuber channels, and the result was a small rise in sales that helped to increase the reviews more. That item was a success.

Create Bundles

If you're purchasing in wholesale, there's a good chance you're buying products that are similar or even work together quite well. In this event, you are given the ability to create a "bundle" product, create the listing for it, and probably offer a pretty decent deal when considering the prices of the items individually. For example, if you're selling cameras, you can bundle a camera with a carrying case. You could also create an even better bundle that comes with a camera, carrying case, extra lens, and a cleaning kit. If that wasn't enough, you can offer a third bundle option for the same products that also includes a tri-pod. By bundling items, you're offering convenience and a slight discount on the price of items that would often be purchased at the same time anyway.

Bundle listings come with another added benefit. Because you'll have to create the product listing yourself, there won't be other sellers offering the same exact bundle (at least not at first, it is possible someone would try to copy your bundle and use your product listing to sell it). At the same time, this is going to include additional work. Not only will you need to produce the listing's description, you'll need to do so in a way that helps sell the items as a package. Additionally, you'll have to produce the product images, and if you want to be fancy, you may need to produce a demonstration video as well. There are a lot of perks to having this much control over a product that's being sold, but it does incur the extra work.

In the event that you're handling private label items, this process should actually be rather simple. Because you'll already have listing copy written for each item, you can use some of the content that is already created to put together your new product listing. Additionally, you will have total control over the price differences between buying the items separately and buying them together. The great thing is that you can create as many bundle variations as you want without actually buying any new products.

While bundling may not seem like a huge scaling effort, the fact of the matter is that it helps to advertise all of the items, offers obvious value (if priced accordingly), and creates another point of contact with potential customers. If it offers good value, receives good reviews, and typically remains available for sale (not running out of stock often), a bundle can easily become one of your bestselling listings.

Set Goals

One of the most important steps in scaling any business is to set goals and work hard until you reach them. Having a goal leads to the development of a plan, and a plan leads to execution. A realistic goal starting out creates a celebration-worthy milestone in your business. If your goal is to make $1,000 in a month, how many of X products must you buy, and how many must you sell, to reach that goal? As you learn what sells, and thus what to buy, these goals become easier to meet and expand upon.

Keep Records

On a similar train of thought, how can you really plan and expand if you aren't taking the time to keep records of your expenses, earnings, items that sell well, items that sit around too long, etc.? Not only does keeping good records make tax time a heck of a lot easier, but it gives you a full picture of what is working and what isn't. Understanding your business from a mathematical standpoint is a must if you have any expectations of growing it to a sizable income stream. If keeping records is difficult for you, seek out help on accounting.

Take Calculated Risks, Try New Things

This is probably the hardest thing for people looking to scale their Amazon FBA-based businesses, but sometimes if an opportunity arises, it is time to take a chance on it. You should definitely still do your research, but sometimes the window of opportunity is short and hesitating too long means you may have missed out on a golden chance. Not every risk is so huge that it will bankrupt you, even if you do ultimately lose money, and not taking risks means you can expect your profits to taper off. Perhaps $1,000-$2,000 per month is enough for you and the risk seems unnecessary, but very few people have made it big without risking their time, money, and occasionally their peace of mind.

Chapter 11: Advertising on Amazon

Are you selling an item new to Amazon's marketplace? If you need to create exposure and traction for an item, advertising it may be the answer. Amazon's Sponsored Products program enables sellers, brand owners, and manufacturers to advertise their Buy Box-eligible listings. If the ads work well for you, they can help buyers find your products and increase your sales. By default, your advertising fees will be deducted from your selling account.

The ads are shown to customers who are searching or browsing similar items on Amazon's website. For example, as shown above, a recent search for the word "drill" displayed two advertisements for sponsored listings at the top of Amazon's search results.

The ads can also appear prominently on the item detail pages for similar products, as shown below.

Sponsored Products is a pay-per-click program, which means you'll pay a fee each time a customer clicks on your ad. The display of your ad results from an auction of your keyword bids against competing advertisers bidding on the same keywords. If the customer clicks on your ad, they're transferred to the detail page of the product you're advertising. If the ad is shown to a customer who doesn't click on the ad, you pay nothing.

Your product must be occupying the Buy Box in order for your ad to display.

Creating a Sponsored Products campaign

To begin, hover over the Advertising tab at Seller Central and select Campaign Manager from the drop-down menu. Specify your campaign's budget and duration. You can target your ads in two different ways: Automatic targeting, where Amazon places your ads in all relevant customer searches based on your product information, or Manual targeting, which displays your ads when a customer's search matches keywords you specify.

Next, indicate your default bid, which is the maximum price you're willing to pay for each click.

Here are some average winning cost-per-click bids by product category:

Understanding Campaign performance

You should evaluate your campaigns at least a couple of times per week to make sure your ad dollars are being spent effectively. Hover over the Advertising tab at Seller Central and select Campaign Manager from the drop-down menu. On the right side of the page you can adjust the time period from which to display the following metrics:

• Spend: The amount you have paid for clicks on your ads.

• Sales: The total product sales resulting from clicks. Results are based on sales of advertised SKUs plus the sales of other SKUs attributed to clicks on ads. (Sales may take 48 hours to be reflected in reports.)

• ACoS: Cost of advertising per sale. The lower the ACoS the better, because it indicates you're spending less of your sales revenue on advertising.

The two key considerations for campaigns are margins and repeat sales. How much of your profit margin on a product are you willing to spend in advertising? Fifty percent? More than 50 percent? Would you spend even more if you were certain that every 25 sales resulted in two repeat purchases during the next 90 days.

To view the performance of each ad, click on the ad group name in Campaign Manager. You'll see each product in the ad group and their following metrics:

impressions (the number of times your ad was shown), clicks, spend, sales and ACoS.

Using manual targeting for a campaign

There are two ways of targeting ads: automatic targeting and manual targeting. A good way to get started is with automatic targeting, in which Amazon matches your ad to relevant customer searches, and you set a single bid. This way, you'll get results from a broad range of customer searches.

Manual targeting gives you more control. You select the keywords you want to use, and adjust your bids based on each keyword's performance. You can use the keywords that were most successful from your automatic campaigns.

To launch your first manual targeting campaign, you'll need to decide which product(s) you want to promote, what your budget will be, the keywords you'll use, and your bids for those keywords.

Understanding keyword match type

Each keyword is a word—or a series if words—you bid on in Campaign Manager to target specific customer searches. There are three different types of keyword matching: broad, phrase, and exact:

Broad match: Your ad can appear whenever a customer searches with any word in your key phrase, in any order. This is the default and reaches the widest audience and results in the most clicks.

Phrase match: Your ad appears when a customer searches for your exact keyword phrase but perhaps with some more words at the beginning and/or end. This is more restrictive and results in fewer clicks than a broad match, but allows for more exact targeting of your ad.

Exact match: The most restrictive option. Your ads are shown only when a customer searches for your exact keyword phrase. For example, if your keyword is "men's hats" your ad will show only for a search for "men's hats." A search for "hats for men" will not show your ad. You might decide to bid higher for an exact match because you are more certain that a customer is using exactly the search phrase you are targeting.

You can evaluate the performance of your ad campaigns by requesting a Campaign Performance Report. At Seller Central, over the Reports tab and select Advertising Reports from the drop-down menu.

Chapter 12: Monitoring product and your business

Now that you're successfully shifting and selling your product... you've now become a real business!! Congratulations to you!

But there's a lot more. You need to declare yourself as a business and complete all the necessary paperwork. You also need to think about paying taxes.

There's a good chance you'll be thinking about a trademark for your brand. If you are managing to sell internationally, you'll find there's even more you'll need to do. All of this is a hassle, and to a certain extent, you shouldn't be wasting time doing it when you should be marketing yourself.

But now isn't the time to despair, because you can get this done quickly. We'll now take a look at the path which has the least resistance for you to become a registered business (most simply). We'll also see how you can organize your bank accounts, and make doing taxes easy when it's time.

Business Structuring

At some point, you're going to need to structure and make sure your business is registered. This isn't as complicated as it sounds. When you first start a business, and you're not selling a lot of product, you haven't got much to do regarding this.

There's no need to incorporate or register yourself as an LLC; you can do this in the future. All you need in the beginning is to be a sole proprietorship. This is a legal status which gives access to various business services and practices.

When you are a sole proprietorship, you are allowed to get an EIN, or an employment identification number. This allows you the reporting of your income, and to obtain benefits such as a business checking account and a business credit card. A sole proprietorship will enable you to use the Amazon tax services. This gives you all you need to help run a successful business on Amazon.

It's straightforward to register for a sole proprietorship, and if you go to the state's Department of Revenue, you can find directions on how to complete the process. Most of which can be completed online. Instead of searching your state's website, you can just Google your state and "sole proprietorship," and you'll be directed to the registration page.

Furthermore, a sole proprietorship will apply to any business you run. So, even if you sell outside of Amazon, you'll have something of value when you register for your sole proprietorship. This is one element you should do as soon as you see your volumes increase.

If you need assistance to register for a sole proprietorship, you can use LegalZoom or Nolo, who carry out the registration on your behalf. You need to complete a few forms, and they'll check them then forward to the relevant agencies. You will then receive your completed documents. These sites are great time savers.

Trademarks and Patents

Patents can help you protect intellectual property. If you introduce a product which has a new feature that's never been seen before, you will patent those features. For many of the products on Amazon, these are the same as others sellers, so a patent won't be required.

Trademarks protect logos, slogans, and brand names. It's good to know that nobody can use any branding you've created. Being truthful here; you probably don't need a trademark, either. At the start, you don't need a trademark, but if you begin making several thousand dollars a month in profit, this might be an appropriate time to do so.

A brand is worth nothing unless it is recognized and you've done the marketing. So, be sure to focus on your launch, and focus on maintaining sales and reviews. On top of that, focus on your reaching out to old and new customers, and to make sure you're running a quality business, overall. Always be professional in your dealings.

Income Tax

Nobody likes to pay income tax, but we all need to do it. Remember, if you're paying taxes, it can show you're making money!

There are ways which you can save time when doing this, and some straightforward things are: getting a business checking account, and a business credit card. With this, you don't need to go through any personal accounts to figure out which payments and receipts are private, and which are for your business.

Once you have your business account, you might want to sign up for a PayPal business account and then redirect Amazon and PayPal to those accounts.

You can hire someone to complete your taxes for you, and a personal accountant can save a lot of time, although there is a cost. A separate way is using a service like Greenback, and with this, you can automate your tax filing. Many services cost, but it can be worth it when they show you what you can claim as expenses, and what you are able to use and re-invest when running your business.

International Sellers

You don't need to live in the US to sell on Amazon.com. You can check a list of countries where you can sell from, and if you live in one of these, you're permitted to be an international seller.

There are a few things needed to be an international seller. First, you need a US-based phone number, a mailing address in the US, and a US bank account. You can obtain a phone number through Skype, a US address with myUS.com, and a US bank account at Payoneer.

All this comes with a cost, but, it can be a worthy price to pay to participate in a market as large as Amazon.

In turn, you could set up business via LegalZoom. This can save a lot of effort. Just contact them, and give them the name of your company and provide a little more information, and they can do the rest for you. Time saved here can be enlightening; I think that's the best word.

Chapter 13: Frequently asked questions

What does Fulfillment by Amazon represent?

Fulfillment by Amazon (FBA) is a very interesting option provided by this platform, which can help merchants boost their business by taking advantage of Amazon's expertise and resources, fast, free and trustworthy shipment, and outstanding customer support services. By choosing this option, you can send your inventory to the platform's warehouses (fulfillment centers) so that they can be stored over there and then leave everything to Amazon, including the picking, packing, and shipping of your customers' orders.

FBA is eligible for all the product categories and subcategories showing up on the Amazon Seller account. It is also available for any reseller who is curious to try it. The maximum weight limit for this program is 30 kilograms per product, so this is a requirement you need to know right from the start. You can test how your products are selling on Amazon, as well as send plenty of them to the fulfillment centers because you don't have to pay for anything upfront. You merely have to spend on their services that you use at the end of the month or when you make a sale.

What exactly is the Amazon Seller Central?

This is the type of account used by merchants, brands or sellers to manage and list their inventory on Amazon.

How to open an Amazon Seller Central account?

You need to establish the steps to follow when opening such an account:

• Select the products that you want to sell

• Visit services.amazon.com or sellercentral.amazon.com and click "Sell" on the main Amazon page.

• Select between the Professional and Individual selling plans.

• Register for the Amazon Seller account.

• Manage your account and list your products.

What are the fees involved when creating the Amazon Seller account?

When selecting the selling plan, you should be able to see the prices of both plans easily. The Individual account costs $0.99, while the Professional one amounts to $39.99. These are both monthly fees, and you are charged 30 days after the registration process.

Is it possible to create an Amazon Selling account for free?

Unfortunately, this is not an option on this platform because you need to choose between an Individual or Professional account.

What do I have to do in order to comply with Amazon's return policy?

Amazon will ask you to provide the following methods for returns:

- a return address;

- a prepaid return level; and

- a full refund without asking for the product to be returned.

How do consumers recognize the Fulfillment by Amazon products on the platform?

These products have the "Fulfillment by Amazon" logo, which provides the customers with the information that support service, returns, packing, and delivery are handled by Amazon.

How to label individual products?

When you wish to add your listings on the platform, you will be faced with a decision that can influence your further success on Amazon. To be precise, you have to select the labelling option, whether you want to send the products using EAN or UPC barcodes (these products fall into the Commingled Inventory or Stickerless category), or label the products properly (Labeled Inventory) to hide the original barcode completely. Commingled Inventory can be combined with other inventories from different merchants; that's why your customers might get products from different resellers, which may or may not have the same features as yours. Amazon will not open the boxes to check which product is the right one and from which merchant it has come from to ensure the authenticity of the merchandise. The Stickerless option, on the other hand, only refers to the products, not to the delivery. Although it may be a bit time-consuming and complicated, you may need to label the items well to protect your inventory and make sure that your customers are getting what they have ordered.

How to print labels for your own products?

When you are adding new products (inventory) from your Seller Central account (you will need to go into "Inventory Amazon Fulfils" and then "Send/replenish inventory") or just preparing an inventory, you are entering something called "shipping workflow." It will provide extra guidance on how to prepare your inventory to be shipped to Amazon's warehouses, thus giving you the option to customize the shipment considering the selections that you make during each step. At one point, you will be prompted to choose the labelling option and allow you to print your unit labels from the shipping workflow directly. These tags will include details like the product title, which can prove to be very helpful when it comes to matching the label with the right product. You need a printer and blank adhesive papers to print such labels, which can be found on the Amazon website or any store that sells office supplies.

Is there a possibility for Amazon to add the labels on your products?

This is a possible option, especially when you are entering the shipping workflow guide. You can simply select Amazon Label Service when prompted with the labelling options. This is a valid solution if you find the private label process too complicated and time-consuming.

How to pack products when sending them to Amazon?

You can find two different types of packing products before sending them to Amazon's warehouses below.

• Individually packed goods means that every box contains one or few units, depending on conditions and quantities.

• Packing items in a case is an option that will allow the merchant to place the products with the same SKU and condition into one box. The boxes will have the same quantity and the same item in them. When Amazon receives these boxes, they will only scan one item from the box and place the whole thing in your inventory. Amazon does not need to scan all the items, considering they are all the same.

When the reseller sends the products to Amazon, they can only be sent using one type of packing per shipment. Although they will be added to the inventory, if the merchant has individually packed items and cases with packed items, he or she will need to send them separately to Amazon.

How to choose a shipping method and carrier to send your inventory to Amazon?

The starting point of creating a new shipment is the "Send/replenish inventory" tab, which is present in the "Inventory Amazon Fulfils" section of your account. It is also possible when you have a work-in-progress inventory and you use the "shipping workflow" tool. By using the latter, you will receive step-by-step instructions on how to prepare your merchandise to be sent over to Amazon, including details about customizing your shipment according to the selections that you make at each step. One of them will allow you to choose from the shipping methods below:

• Small Parcel Deliveries (SPDs) represent individually packed and labelled products (one product per box), all prepared to be shipped.

• Less-Than-Truckload (LTL) shipments are, in fact, a mixed delivery because it contains pallets and individually boxed products. In this case, some of the products may be sent to different destinations, different warehouses.

• Full Truckload (FTL) also combines full pallets and individually packed products. The difference, however, is that the whole merchandise is going to one warehouse.

The FBA terms and conditions apply to all products that you send to and are meant to be sold on Amazon, regardless of the shipping method that you select. You can find more details related to how the platform receives and routes your products if you check these terms and conditions.

You can also choose a different carrier, other than the one provided by Amazon. Costs can be higher in this case, but if you do want to go ahead with this option, you will need to work with a trusted carrier that is capable of providing you with valuable information like a valid tracking number for SPD, the pro/freight bill number for FTL or LTL deliveries, and the bill of lading (BOL).

You can't send the inventory to Amazon using a privately-owned car, however. It can only be done by a registered carrier.

How to create shipping labels?

The shipping workflow is a sequence and tool where you can simply choose the type of labels that you want to have (if there is any). When selecting Small Parcel

Delivery (SPD), you will be prompted to print shipping labels (just one per box) and packing slips. You will also need to place the packing slip inside the box, on the top side, so that it can be seen immediately after being opened at the Amazon's warehouse. The information that you should include are the destination and return addresses, while the label should be positioned just outside the sealed box as an addition to labels added by the carrier.

If you select Less-Than-Truckload, you still need to print a label per each box, which has to be placed outside of it so it can be seen when unwrapping the pallet. On the pallets, the tags have to be placed in a top-center position on each side (on the stretched wrap).

Adhesive labels can be found at any office supplies store or on Amazon.

Is it possible to arrange a shipment of inventory directly from an overseas supplier?

This is not an acceptable option because Amazon can't be used as the final address, importer or consignee when sending products from overseas. In this case, merchants will have to make the necessary arrangement to import and clear the shipment of customs. Only after doing this that they can send the inventory to Amazon's warehouses.

How to notify Amazon in advance regarding the products that I'm sending to them?

You have three options of sending products over to Amazon: Small Parcel Delivery (SPD), Less-Than-Truckload (LTL), and Full Truckload (FTL). For the last two choices, you will need to arrange delivery appointments; otherwise, the fulfillment centers may decline your shipment. In order to arrange a delivery appointment with the warehouse where you want to send the inventory, you will need first to download the Fulfillment by Amazon booking form, fill it, and email it to the carrier. In this form, you will have to place the ZIP code (you can find it in the Shipping Queue section of your account). Once the carrier has received your form, they will send it to the Amazon's Fulfillment Center to schedule the best delivery timing. It usually takes around 24 hours for the warehouse to reply back to the carrier with a confirmation for the delivery time.

How safe are Amazon's fulfillment centers?

You simply can't imagine better storage conditions for your inventory than the fulfillment centers owned by Amazon. hey are very secure and have the optimal temperature to keep your merchandise safe and in perfect condition. In many cases, picking, packing, and shipping tasks are done automatically, so they are all processed very fast. Some of the features of these establishments are 24/7 security staff, fully automated and wireless order tracking, climate-controlled storage units, and secured areas.

How are the feedbacks handled for any sold FBA product?

Leaving feedback is just a very powerful tool that buyers use on this platform to talk about a product. Amazon doesn't filter the feedback left by any buyer on FBA orders even if it's not related to the fulfillment part of the order.

In the case of poorly managed fulfillment caused by Amazon, which is reflected in the feedback left by the shopper, Amazon will be checking if: 1) the product in question is fulfilled by the platform; 2) the purchase rating of the buyer is between 1 and 3; 3) the buyer confirmed that the product is "Item as described"; and 4) the product did not arrive on time (according to the buyer).

Is Amazon taking care of refunds and customer returns for the FBA products?

Yes, but this is only valid for products sold on the platform! Amazon has its own policy when it comes to returns, and it is all included in the FBA Service Terms and Selling on Amazon Service Terms. They can merely process refunds and returns according to this policy. Any customer interested in returning an item that has been purchased from Amazon can check the Online Return Support Center where they can find contact details for the channel. Also, there is a designated Returns Center where all the customers who want to return a product will be directed. If it was not sold on the Amazon market, the merchant is solely responsible for the refund and return process.

What is the procedure in case of returns?

Well, this depends on the marketplace where the product was sold. If it was purchased on Amazon, and if they establish if the returned product can still be sold (meaning, it needs to have the same condition as before the sale), they will simply put the item back in your inventory and mark it as available for sale. If the merchandise is not in its original condition, Amazon will not place it back on sale, and the product will show up as "unfulfillable" in your account. At this point, you have 90 days to inform Amazon whether you want the product returned back to you or you just want it disposed of. If you fail to comply, Amazon will simply return the product to you.

In the case of a product being sold on a different platform, but it's fulfilled by Amazon, they will just send the product directly to you.

How to find the products which have been returned to Amazon and refunded to the customer?

When you use FBA with your Amazon Seller Central account, you can discover a reporting section from which you can download the report with returns requested by your customers.

If you are curious about refunds processed to your customers, you will need to check the payments sections of your account.

Can you consider Amazon as a search engine?

As it turns out, this platform also acts as a search engine. There are plenty of situations in which the customers of this marketplace have the option to compare prices and find items that they might want to buy. With Alexa, for instance, the buyers have the option to use voice search instead of typing the query.

Also, the platform can also be utilized to find out what new products are selling online.

Is Amazon's search algorithm updated regularly?

Nobody outside of Amazon knows for sure how often the search algorithm changes on this platform. Luckily for all the merchants selling over here, the current algorithm is quite stable, so you can optimize your content even if the system doesn't really change.

What does Amazon SERP stand for?

Every time you are searching for products on this platform, you can type in some keywords, and it acts as a search engine and displays a list of results. SERP is just the term used for these results because it literally means the search engine results page.

Conclusions

Starting an Amazon FBA business is not as hard as it may sound, and the work that goes into it is generally easy. While there are some steps you need to cover to ensure you are doing it properly, having it done right will keep you earning profit time and time again.

There are a few areas that you need to consider when you are building your Amazon FBA business, as you truly are building a business and you need to ensure that you run it as such. You should always be professional and ensure that you or your outsourcing is vigilant about keeping up with everything.

This book covers the basics of what FBA is and how you, as a seller, can use it to your advantage. For the exact details about FBA and to know about the latest advancements, visit Amazon's website or contact Amazon's incredible customer service. Amazon values its clients and sellers equally.

Amazon FBA is truly a powerful business to get into. These days, everyone does their shopping online. While brick and mortar stores are wonderful, having an online business is easy, and gives you wide open access to a much larger audience. Getting into this business is something that will serve you for years to come, as long as you maintain it properly.

The next step for you is to decide what product you are going to take to market. Then, you can start finding a supplier and either have the product made for you or shipped for you. At that point, you can start marketing your product. Then, you want to build a powerful advertisement page on Amazon and ensure that your keywords are proper.

You can go virtually anywhere with your business on Amazon FBA, which is one of the best parts of it. You can expand your business as large as you want and earn as much as you'd like simply by repeating the process within' this book over and over and over again.

All the best in your new Amazon FBA business!